P

MW01148099

"Being Catholic in an imperfect world comes with its own unique set of challenges. Whether you encounter rebellious teens, unsupportive extended family, mental illness, a contentious marriage, or other crises of faith, morality, and psychology, *Family Faith Under Fire* has just what you need. In his usual no-nonsense, practical, and humorous style, Dr. Ray Guarendi offers wisdom and insight from an authentically Catholic perspective and with the voice of experience. An easy, entertaining, and enlightening read for Catholics from all walks of life!"

—Danielle Bean, publisher, *Catholic Digest,*
and author, *Momnipotent*

"Dr. Ray Guarendi combines his keen intellect, his years of experience as a clinical psychologist, and his hands-on experience as a father of ten to create a book that is as wise as it is warm. *Family Faith Under Fire* is a must-read book for anyone who faces the daunting task of evangelizing the toughest crowd of all: your own family."

—Jennifer Fulwiler, author, *Something Other Than God*

"Most Catholics have no problem practicing their faith ... while they're in church. Once Mass is over, however, it gets much more challenging. In his book *Family Faith Under Fire*, Dr. Ray Guarendi addresses several of the most common difficulties that arise from living the Catholic Faith at home, in the workplace, and in the real world. In a clear and succinct manner (with lots of humor thrown in), he tells us what we need to know in order to really live our faith 24-7. Highly recommended!"

—Gary Zimak, speaker and author, *Faith, Hope, and Clarity*

"Dr. Ray has done it again! His list of snappy (but charitable) answers to rude questions is worth the price of the book. But there's so much more."

— **Mike Aquilina, author, _Yours Is the Church_**

"Dr. Ray gives practical spiritual advice while answering tough questions concerning raising children in the Faith. A true guidebook of responses and actions to help parents and grandparents persevere in love while maintaining and passing on truth."

— **Julie Dortch Cragon, author,**
**_Amazing Graces: The Blessings of Sacramentals_**

"Who wouldn't benefit from a healthy dose of Dr. Ray? His simple, straightforward insights are an antidote to the friction and the frazzle in our families. Clear, concrete guidance for the confused. Faithful, funny direction for the distraught. And just plain good advice for Catholic parents of all shapes and sizes. Thanks, Dr. Ray. I needed that!"

— **Gina Loehr, author, _Saint Francis, Pope Francis_**

"Do you get upset about faith-related conflicts with your family and friends? Dr. Ray's book is the best I've ever read about such problems. It is not only inspiring but also sensible and humorous. You will find surprising answers to questions you thought there were no answers for."

— **Ronda Chervin, Ph.D., professor of philosophy,**
**Holy Apostles College and Seminary**

"This book is down to earth, practical, funny, and a breath of fresh air. Thanks Dr. Ray, from a father of nine!"

— **Chris Padgett, coauthor,**
**_Holy Marriage, Happy Marriage_**

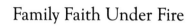

Family Faith Under Fire

Other books by Dr. Ray Guarendi
from EWTN Publishing:

*Raising Upright Kids in an Upside-Down World:
Defying the Anti-Parent Culture*

*Jesus, the Master Psychologist: Listen to Him*

*Thinking Like Jesus: The Psychology of a Faithful Disciple*

*Adoption: Should You, Could You, and Then What?
Straight Answers from a Psychologist and Adoptive Father of Ten*

*Living Calm: Mastering Anger and Frustration*

*Taught by Ten: A Psychologist Father Learns from His Ten Children*

*Simple Steps to a Stronger Marriage*

*Standing Strong: Good Discipline Makes Great Teens*

Dr. Ray Guarendi

# Family Faith Under Fire
## Practical Answers to
## Everyday Challenges

EWTN Publishing, Inc.
Irondale, Alabama

EWTN Publishing, Inc.

5817 Old Leeds Road, Irondale, AL 35210

Distributed by Sophia Institute Press, Box 5284, Manchester, NH 03108.

paperback ISBN 978-1-68278-269-9

ebook ISBN 978-1-68278-270-5

Library of Congress Control Number: 2024942545

First printing

*To Al Kresta,*
*my dear friend and mentor*
*and a man of God*

# Contents

# Introduction

"Clinical psychologist" is my professional title. My education could rightly be called secular. The schooling I received was that standard in a nonreligious university program. My instructors pretty much avoided touching on traditional religion and morals. While acknowledging that many clients did live by some religion, they advised maintaining a dogmatically neutral moral stance. Though I practiced my Catholic Faith back then, I would practice psychology as I was taught.

Some years after graduating, I drifted from the Church. I didn't head toward hostile anti-religion, with a "Christian beliefs are pre–psychological enlightenment" mindset. Rather, I took a more self-affirming attitude: God sees things in the same ways that I do.

Thank God, He doesn't. By His mercy, I scratched and clawed my way back into the Church. While I still practiced psychology with a general population, more Christians began seeking my guidance. They expressed a trust that I would understand and respect their core beliefs. It was a trust they were finding less and less elsewhere.

Matters of faith and psychology routinely meet. Parenting, emotions, anxieties, relationships—all intersect with the central question for religious people: How can I live my faith better, in thought and action, especially with those closest to me?

This book collects those questions that I am most often asked regarding issues of faith and family. How do I get my kids, and myself, to be more attentive at prayer? Why are my children resisting the Faith? Why did my children leave the Church when they became adults? How do I best respond to criticisms of my religion? How do I protect my children's innocence in a culture that morally disagrees with me? What do I say to loved ones whose thinking about religion is confused? What do I do when my spouse is threatened by my faith?

Some of these questions I've grappled with personally. I suspect you have too. I hope you will find here some answers to help you "run with perseverance the race that is set before us" (Heb. 12:1).

Part 1

# Mass Resistance

God has given us the Mass for our infinite well-being. It is good for us in the short-term — life here — and for the long-term — life hereafter.

Even so, not everyone understands the worth of the Mass. Just because something is for our immeasurable benefit doesn't mean we will want it. Some wayward children resist the arms of their loving Father.

# A Choice for Life

*Dear Dr. Ray,*

*My daughter, age fourteen, is starting to resist going to church. I worry that if I force her, someday she'll reject religion altogether. My mother tells me not to push her, that as she gets older, she'll come around.*

*Waiting*

Here's a child-rearing experiment: From age two forward, do not make Charity do anything against her will. Twinkies or lima beans—her pick. School or television—her preference. Hug her brother or smack him—whatever. She can eat what she wants, sleep when she wants, work how she wants, and visit your mother if she wants.

With each year, will Charity choose more good over bad? Or will she develop into a self-absorbed, unhealthy young adult?

Kids aren't naturally inclined toward what is in their best interest. (Who is?) If they were, how much direction would they need? The whole growing-up process would be far smoother, for us and them. Loving parents use force—not physical but social and moral. They make a child, when judged wise, do what she resists and not do what she wills.

A television show invited me to discuss this topic: Should parents force their values upon their children, or should their children be free to choose their own? It didn't take a shrink to analyze the show's bias.

Your mother sounds as if she is echoing that show. (Do you think she watched it?) That is, one must feel like acting for the act to be genuine. If imposed from the outside, little settles inside. The roots are shallow, easily uprooted.

Some believe this sentiment particularly true for Faith. Teaching anything religious is psychologically acceptable so long as a child remains open, but once closed, religious instruction borders on compulsion. Using this logic, passing on any sort of values would be dependent upon a child's agreeable feelings.

I'll confess, as a forward-looking third grader, that I had little inner motive to master the multiplication tables. Backed by my parents' insistence, Mrs. Becker made me.

Must a parent passively wait until a young person, on his own, feels a God-longing? While children can seek a divine connection solo, those who do so are a minority. The majority are introduced to God early in life, by faith-filled parents, coming to know Him more deeply with maturity.

Is free choice a fair choice? If your daughter one day leaves the Faith, shouldn't she understand what she's leaving? If you allow her to learn by herself, will she stay stuck in youthful ignorance, which may evolve into arrogant ignorance? True freedom begins with knowing what is good to choose.

Teens—and many grown-ups too—have little or no idea of the possible consequences of a bad decision. It is infinitely unwise to allow the immature to decide independently about a matter of infinite importance. And what decision is more consequential than that of moving toward God or away from Him?

A tragic reality: large numbers of young adults who jettison the faith of their childhood. Many proclaim, "I was made to go to church as a kid, so as I got older and on my own, I quit." Decades of doing therapy have taught me that routinely we are unaware of our true motives. "I was made to" is often the spoken rationale for the unspoken "I don't want to anymore." The real reason has little to do with being forced to attend Mass years ago.

Throughout my teens, my mother insisted I visit my ninety-plus-year-old great-aunt, an activity near the bottom of my adolescent to-do list. Did my mother risk making me one day want to shun old people? I don't think she ever worried about that. Or did she show me a side of life I needed to see and wouldn't on my own? Long after I lost Mom as my motivator, I not only visited the elderly but came to appreciate them.

A father told me his teens nagged to sleep in on Sunday mornings rather than get up for Mass. Dad wouldn't hear of it. He knew that something at Mass could somehow touch their souls. One thing for sure: That couldn't happen if they weren't there.

# Dependent Independence

*My twenty-year-old son has returned home from college for the summer and is arguing that he is old enough to decide whether or not to attend Mass. He also tells us he has pretty much stopped going to Mass at school.*

*Still the Parent*

Age entitlement: It's the juvenile mindset that proclaims, "I'm [enter number], so I can [enter perk—date, drive, dress as I wish, buy what I want, set my curfew]." A slew of so-called freedoms are supposed to arrive just because a certain age does. Some of these might arrive—if Forbes buys his own car, covers his own rent, pays his own bills. In short, if he is truly independent.

Your son may have the illusion of full self-determination because, for the better part of the last year or so, he's been playing house at school. But the facts are stubborn: He still relies upon your support. Despite his decree, there are limits to his autonomy, some of which are set by you.

College students drift from Mass for a range of reasons: questions about the Faith, an apathy toward things religious, partying late Saturday and sleeping late Sunday, a newfound sense of adult-hood: "I'm a big boy now, so no more rules, thank you."

Whatever the change in your son's thinking, your thinking remains unchanged: Mass is nonnegotiable. It is a given of his summer home relocation. Otherwise, the perks of twenty-hood (no doubt financed in whole or part by you)—car, computer, cell phone, insurance, haircuts—can be reassessed. After which your son could conclude he went from Disney World to Alcatraz in one short day in May.

If you mandate Mass, are you risking further pushback? (Refer back to the previous chapter, "A Choice for Life.") Could he resent being treated as if he's still under your roof?

Perhaps. A young adult living at home does make some rules trickier to enforce. Nonetheless, living with grown-up children often comes down to taking a stance. Your stance: Our family worships God, and Mass is at the center of our worship.

So your son is in church, but his mind isn't. It is back at school, where he lives free. While you can't do much to stop his journeying mind, you can ensure that his body stays in a holy place. And who knows, every so often his mind and body might connect, giving Mass's grace a chance to connect to him.

Should you decide to let him decide against Mass, will younger siblings be watching, and will they decide that core family standards relax with age? When they reach their brother's age, will they, too, think they've earned the right to opt out of Mass?

On campus, your influence dwindles. Your son is miles beyond your eye- and earshot. Your knowledge of his whereabouts and whoabouts is mostly indirect: grades, billing statements, conduct reports—do colleges do those anymore? Do you have a ten-year-old daughter who can tail him and send back daily reports?

Admit your limits: You can't monitor his Sundays—or any other days, for that matter. But, however much you contribute to tuition, cell phone, car, or cash, you do have long-range leverage. Monetary aid is not automatic but is linked to his honesty and reliability. His promise—and proof—of attending Mass is a small gift for all the goodies you dispense, at home and away.

One father confirmed his son's Sunday itinerary, telling him, "The first time I pick you up from school, I'm going to visit the parish priest and ask if he knows you."

# Touchy Topic

*Dear Dr. Ray,*

*My twenty-three-year-old daughter slowly drifted away from Mass after she moved out on her own. Our relationship is good, but whenever I bring up the subject of Mass, she shuts down. What can I say to persuade her?*

*Stifled*

I can say what not to say: "Did you get to Mass this week?" "Father has been asking where you've been." "The priest at Holy Family near you gives great homilies — and they have donuts after Mass." "When was the last time you saw the inside of a church?"

You gave your daughter a belief system, one that you embrace to this day. She knows exactly your thinking. She lived with it for over two decades, and you've reiterated it many times since she moved out. Those conversations don't end well. And you thought her eye rolls would stop with her teen years.

Has your daughter abandoned her belief in God or the Church? Or has she decided that being at Mass isn't necessary to be a good person or a faithful one. Mass has become a negotiable among her religious practices. Her young independence allows her the freedom to set her own schedule, and weekends are social time. Church has become one place to visit among many.

Some teen rebellion may be lingering, as she sees the Faith as something she has, for now, outgrown. It was something you both shared when she was little, but she's a big girl now.

Your best persuasion is a good relationship. Since you have that, continuing to broach a sore subject may only make it more sore. Your daughter might feel on edge, waiting for you to turn the conversation toward her religious disinterest.

"The parish is having a spaghetti dinner next Saturday after Mass. We can go to Mass first and then eat." "So what do you do now that your Sunday mornings are open?" "Your cousin has returned to church, and she seems so much happier." Subtlety can be pretty obvious.

What drives a parent to visit a topic that gets more raw with each visit?

*The heavy stakes factor.* This is not about what school to attend, what job to seek, or what car to buy—all of which are transient decisions with transient consequences. The faith decision reaches to the very ends of life. If she rejects Mass, what will fall next? The matter is deemed too urgent to stay silent.

*The failure factor.* "How did I fail to impart the Faith?" "What did I miss?" "What could I have done better?"

As we'll address later, such self-blame can be badly misdirected. It can mercilessly corrode a parent's peace, compelling her to keep pushing even though a young adult pushes back harder.

*The rejection factor.* "How can she turn away from something that was once such a big part of who she was? At one time, she wanted to be a nun."

Because the turnabout seems so unexpected, it can't be all that real. It must be a phase, a temporary grab for religious independence.

Perhaps. But for the meanwhile, for whatever reasons, the child-turned-adult has drifted. The more you're convinced, "She just needs to be nudged to come back to who she was," the harder you'll nudge when she doesn't budge.

Do you avoid the subject altogether? Yes and no. Yes, as in, you don't initiate it. Don't advise, push, or argue. You've had plenty of signals: "Mom, don't!"

No, in that, if your daughter initiates it, listen long and hear her out. First, get inside her head and understand. Let her explain her thinking. Hearing herself, she may hear that she's not sounding so enlightened.

Brace yourself for what you might hear. After all, she is twenty-three. Are you now who you were at twenty-three?

# Missing in Action

*Dear Dr. Ray,*

*My husband is a good father but seldom attends church with the family. My twelve-year-old son is asking, "Why do I have to go to church if Dad doesn't?"*

*The Sunday Parent*

If you're asking me how to answer your son, let me ask you, "What do you think I am—a psychologist or something?"

Actually, I am, so I suspect your son's motive is not what he says it is. It is said: Anything—or anyone—can be a justification for something you really don't want to do. If your son is ambivalent about church, Dad may be his nearby rationale.

Why is your son co-opting his father for his cause? For one thing, if he really wanted to attend Mass, he would, no matter what Dad did. For another, he'd probably push Dad to go too. Right now, though, he's asking, "If this is so important, why doesn't Dad think so?" In his eyes, the parent vote is tied at one to one.

Absolutely, a faithful father is a powerful presence, especially for a son. In word and action, he emphasizes that religion is not solely a woman's thing. Still, even if Dad's faith walk is a stumble, you can steadfastly walk your son toward God. Two parents on the same spiritual page is the ideal, but one parent living the Faith is far better than none.

Explain your husband to your son. My guess is that you already have, especially in the car rides to and from Mass. Try something like, "Dad is an adult, and he makes his own decisions. I can't tell Dad what to do about church. You are my son. I am responsible before God to raise you as well as I can. And that means teaching you about Jesus and His Church. When you are an adult, you will make your own decisions. Right now, I must decide what is good for you."

Now I ask you, with such loving, irresistible reasoning, how you could not hear, "Gosh, Mom, I've never looked at it that way before. You are so heavenly connected. That's why you're my teacher, and I'm your disciple. What time is Mass again?"

If your son's main motive is "I don't want to," you won't silence his "Why doesn't Dad?"—however flawless your logic. Nonetheless, you have stated your position clearly. Sometimes that's the best a parent can do.

Next, explain your son to your husband. Make sure he knows that your son is citing him as his reason for resisting Mass. A parent comfortable with his own church reluctance may not be so with his child's. While he opts out of Mass, he may not want his child to.

I taught a Bible study for inmates at a county jail. The guys brought with them diverse upbringings and beliefs. When I'd ask, "Why did you come to the Bible study?" I'd often hear something like "I wasn't raised in any church, but I had an aunt who was really religious, and every once in a while, she'd take me to church with her." The mustard seeds of belief were scattered young, and, though dormant for a time, they sprouted in an adult moved to check out this Christianity thing.

Your son, as he moves into a more masculine adolescence, may not be as attracted to his mother's religious bent. With or without Dad's help, however, you are giving him a look at eternity, something that Dad, at this time, has stopped looking toward.

And who knows? Your faithfulness may eventually open your husband's eyes. As Scripture says, "A little child shall lead them" (Isa. 11:6).

# Imperfect Motivation

*Dear Dr. Ray,*

*My husband attends Mass with me and my two sons, but he says he's doing so for me. I want him to go because of his own beliefs.*

*Dispirited*

Catholic theology talks of "imperfect contrition," sorrow for sins motivated mainly by the fear of punishment—more specifically, Hell. Sorrow for having offended God may be somewhere in the mix, but it is not primary. Although imperfect contrition is not the ideal, it still can invoke God's mercy. It is a starting point to more perfect contrition—motivated by love of God. With time and grace, a self-embracing motive can progress into a God-embracing one.

In marriage counseling, a wife expresses her wish that her husband be more affectionate. He responds that, by nature, he's not an affectionate guy. Yet, for her sake, he'll work on it. In the wife's eyes, this is imperfect affection. Hubby is not being affectionate because he feels it; instead, it's to please her. Still, his motive is honorable. A good spouse regularly steps outside of "who he is" and acts to please the other.

Some couples seek counseling when their marriage is barely breathing. One or both would like to leave. Because of the kids, however, they agree to persevere. The troubled marriage not only survives but heals because one or both spouses work at it for the kids' sake. For a while, the children are the primary reason Mom and Dad stick together, but time allows other reasons to accumulate. When the kids grow up, the parents don't grow apart.

Psychology 101: Motives evolve. A five-year-old doesn't hit his sister because she'll hit him back or because he'll be punished. A ten-year-old doesn't hit his sister because it's wrong. A fifteen-year-old doesn't hit her because she has cute girlfriends. Sometimes motives do regress temporarily on the erratic way to maturity.

Understandably, you want your husband to attend Mass because he loves God. Perhaps that motive is acting somewhat, or he wouldn't accompany you at all. He'd feel the hypocrite. For now, he is at Mass for you and with you. And whether or not he means to, he is placing himself in God's presence. A God-seeking seed may be planted and grow.

What if he loses interest in accompanying you? Don't pressure. Allow him to retreat and restart as he wishes. If he's going to Mass for you, you want him to go willingly.

# Part-Time Religion

*Dear Dr. Ray,*

*My wife divorced me three years ago. We have shared custody of our twelve-year-old son and nine-year-old daughter. Their mother practices little religion. I take the children to church when they are with me, but I worry that their exposure to the Faith is not consistent enough.*

*Weekend Dad*

Bad news and good news. The bad news: Your influence is less now than when you and their mother were together, even if you didn't share the Faith. A spouse present full-time, even in a troubled marriage, almost always has more influence than one present part-time after divorce. That is a sad, unavoidable outcome of a family breakup. Both parents have less parental persuasion. What their kids see, hear, and do in the other house is beyond the parents' reach, for the most part. And if one spouse or both remarry, the dynamics get even more complicated.

The good news. You still can show your kids a Christian life. As the parent who takes the Faith seriously, you can give your children what you can when you can.

Being their father brings an added benefit. One survey found that when both parents attend church with the children, 60 to 80 percent of the children attend church as adults. If only Dad attends with them, the figure remains close to the same. Exactly why isn't clear, but it does underscore a father's role as a spiritual model.

The saying is: Mothers make boys; fathers make men. Your son is watching you. If he sees his father living his Faith both inside and outside the church doors, those doors will open wider for him. Dad doesn't only trudge him to Sunday Mass; he prays by his and his sister's bedsides. Dad reads the Bible in full view of his children. Dad leads mealtime blessings, in restaurants even. Dad doesn't disparage Mom for her lack of religion. In all, Dad is a better father because he is a man of God.

A little girl looks at Daddy through a softer lens. His religious ways make him a warmer person. She can count on him to be there for her. He is her defender, her hero. Never underestimate the appeal of a hero image, particularly one shaped by God's hand. Your faith will speak much more loudly to your daughter because she sees it throughout her childhood.

What does their mother think of your differences? Does she respect your right to teach the children when they are with you? Of course, this would make your life easier. Or does she disagree, even disdain? Does she actively undercut both your religion and your parenting?

Whatever their mother's attitude, you are still the main, perhaps the only, Bible and Church your children see right now. You are giving them the truth, which they may not get anywhere else.

Whether or not your children will embrace the Church as young adults, you can't know. You couldn't know for sure had you and their mother remained one in marriage. What you can know for sure is that you are using your time today to be a faithful father. Your children know that their dad isn't just a religious guy; he also loves them, supports them, and sacrifices for them. And that is a witness well beyond one cut in half.

Part 2

# Attention Deficit

Mass, the summit of Catholic worship, deserves the spiritual best of all who are graced to be present. So why is it so hard to stay consistently present?

From the youngest, controlled disruption is about the best we can expect. Older kids no longer submarine beneath the pews or wail at ninety-two decibels. Mostly they stay still and silent, sometimes too much so.

We Mass-goers can give the impression that we're one with what's happening. Yet our minds can be off somewhere, far from the sanctuary.

Fortunately, there are ways to keep the little ones physically oriented toward the altar and us bigger ones spiritually oriented toward God.

# Mass Maneuvers

*Dear Dr. Ray,*

*How can I get my fourteen-month-old to behave at Mass?*

*Crying Mom*

Can you ask an easier question? Such as "How can I get the earth to spin in the reverse direction?" Or "How can I build a cold fusion nuclear reactor in my backyard?" Or "How can I get my husband to pick up his dirty socks?"

Allow me to answer your question with *my* questions. (We shrink types do that when we have no ready answer.)

What makes you think you can participate peacefully in anything with a fourteen-month-old—for a full hour, no less?

What exactly do you mean by "behave"? No whining? No audible fussing? No playing "Look how cute I am" during the homily with the two retirees one row back? How about if we think of behaving as causing minimal disruption? A savvy parent sometimes has to relax her definitions.

Toddlers are old enough to create relentless turbulence but not quite old enough to learn from discipline, which only makes them louder.

Maneuvering Mass with a toddler is a little like street police work. Spells of relative calm are unpredictably shattered by chaos. Your goal is not to make it without incident to the "Go in peace." It is to increase the peace between incidents, looking to the day your child will reverently absorb the celebration—somewhere around age twenty. Just kidding—sort of.

Try as I might, I seldom reach 100 percent presence at Mass. Something or someone always distracts me. Usually it's somebody's child.

To prolong the calm periods—there's no getting full calm at fourteen months—bring along some toddler tranquilizers: a cloth book or two (paper rustles and melts in the mouth); something to suck on, chew on, or drink from—a pacifier (now there's a misnomer), a bottle, a sippy cup, his toes; a soft toy, stuffed animal, favorite blanket. Leave at home anything that uses batteries or makes a sound when dropped from nine inches or less. His shoes?

Travel light. Don't haul in half of Faith's bedroom, Grandma's Christmas Toys "R" Us warehouse, and the Bible Buffet. More stuff only supplies more material for disruption. Follow the airlines' rule: Try to get everything into one small carry-on.

What about sitting in the front so little John Paul can be mesmerized by the priest's movements? That's one choice. But can you make it to Mass early enough to snag the front pew? Little kids move in a time warp. You may have to sleep on the church steps the previous night.

If you don't occupy the first pew, your child will see mostly backsides, unless you hold him for an hour. Even with that, all the distracting faces sit behind.

Better to plant yourself toward the back. If your child acts up and you can't soothe or distract him, the farther back you're seated, the better. It's a long mile from the front pew to the vestibule.

Dozens of eyes will follow you and your crabby kid, with thoughts like "Why didn't she just sit in the cry room in the first place?" or "Mine knew better than to act like that." Walking a tightrope across Niagara Falls carrying a cougar would seem the shorter trek. Borrowing the Master's words in the wedding parable, "Give place to this man" (the one with the well-behaved kids), and "take the lowest place" (Luke 14:9). From the rear pews, sanctuary is only a few short feet away. But don't let John Paul roam around the foyer. He's to be in your arms—with no books, toys, computer, cell phone, or Big Wheel. Show him that it's better to be back inside.

If you're wanting to immerse John Paul in the Mass at a young age, you may be a shade early, developmentally speaking. Not until age three or so will much register in his memory. Your immediate goal, wherever you sit, is to immerse him in pleasant preoccupations. And if the Mass breaks in here and there, count your blessings.

Did I answer your question? I did, and I didn't. No, there are no strategies this side of Heaven to guarantee hour-long toddler cooperation, except sleep—his, not yours. Yes, there are strategies to keep you both inside semi-peacefully for longer periods—your aim for this Church calendar year.

I think I read somewhere that the world record for a parent and toddler coming and going during one Mass is seventeen times. In defense of the parent, it was an Easter Vigil, with the two-dozen-plus Scripture readings and eleven Baptisms.

# The Good Young Days

*Dear Dr. Ray,*

*As a toddler, my son was much better behaved during Mass than he is now at age three.*

*No Sign of Peace*

Managing a one-year-old involves three S's—supervise, sidetrack, and stop. Managing a three-year-old adds a fourth S: standard discipline—expectations backed by consequences. It's an addition helpful to both parent and child.

Near age twenty months, our oldest son, Andrew, began to consider himself a bit too grown-up for his little-kid bedtime. One evening, at peak bedtime bad time, I hustled him to the corner for the very first time in his life. Watching, my wife chided me. When I defended myself with "He needed to be put there," she replied, "I know, but I wanted to do it."

Apparently, following ten feet behind Andrew all day every day while I was safely ensconced somewhere writing parenting books had readied her for the day, or night, she could put more discipline oomph into her words. She had earned the privilege.

Your son is more willful now than he was two years ago. That's pretty typical. But you have more discipline flexibility now than you did two years ago. That's pretty positive.

Begin with tried-and-true toddler tactics. Let Pius keep company with a small picture book, stuffed animal, or toy. These don't compete with the Mass. They settle Pius. And settled is a forerunner to better behaved.

Accept forward orientation: Allow Pius some latitude in where he looks, sits, stands, or even sleeps, as long as most of the time he's oriented toward the front of the church. No climbing over, under, around, or through the pew. No playing hide-and-seek with the five-year-old three seats back. Proper body disposition precedes proper behavior disposition.

A few older folks—those who brought young kids to Mass forty-five years ago—might think Pius is cute. But "cute" fades fast with obnoxious repetition. Head to the vestibule at the first squeak of trouble. Don't wait for the commotion to get loud enough to drown out the priest. You're not admitting defeat or rewarding Pius with a get-out-of-Mass-free card. Yours is prudent parenting, while protecting those around you from a near occasion of sin.

Seek a sanctuary (not *the* sanctuary) for discipline. The vestibule probably has a bathroom, and bathrooms have corners. Your car comes standard with a car seat; ignore Pius until he settles.

Heading to Grandma's after Mass? Her place has lots of corners, though Grandma might decry their being so misused on her misunderstood grandson. (Are these the same people who raised us?)

Home will dramatically expand your discipline options. But would you be waiting too long? Shouldn't disciplining young children follow closely after the misbehavior?

Mostly that's so with children younger than your son. At three and a half, he's capable of linking what he did then to what you're doing now, especially if you remind him, "Pius, you didn't listen to Mommy at church. Now you have to put your head down at the table."

For multiple disruptions, try multiple consequences. "No cookie today because you ate a page out of the missalette. Your bedtime doggie is on top of the refrigerator because you stepped on your sister's head to climb over the seat. And you're not getting a red Corvette at your high school graduation; we had to leave Mass three times."

Voice your expectations before Mass. "Pius, if you bang the kneeler up and down, when we get home you'll go sit on your bed." Are you planting ideas into his liturgical repertoire? He doesn't need your ideas. He has more than enough of his own.

Will post-Mass discipline sour Pius on the Mass? Does any discipline anywhere risk a psychological backlash? If you discipline Pius at Grandma's, will he avoid Grandma? If you require a bedtime, will he hate his bed, bedroom, and sunset? All discipline takes place somewhere about something, typically many times. Such is the reality of childhood — indeed, adulthood.

Pius may be rowdy, but he's not dumb. He shouldn't need too many weeks to learn better behavior or, at the least, to fall asleep faster. Teaching him the beauty of the Mass begins with not permitting him to be ugly during it.

# I'm Conscious

*Dear Dr. Ray,*

*My sixteen-year-old son seems oblivious during Mass. He doesn't sing, seldom responds, and does more staring off than anything else.*

*Watching*

It's an irony of age. Little kids get manic at Mass; big kids get comatose. Little kids are in perpetual motion; big kids go through the motions. The transformation evolves subtly over a decade or so. Whatever happened to the seven-year-old who used to play Mass in the living room?

What accounts for this all-too-common teen picture? Does it have something to do with the nature of adolescence itself—that is, an apathy toward the things of grown-ups, a.k.a. old people? Is it a stage, something that will subside with time? Is it rebellion? My parents want me here more than I do, so I'll be here—kind of.

Any of these can be present. Still, even taken together, they don't fully explain this mass Mass apathy. For that, another factor is at work, one fueled by adrenaline. The typical teen's lifestyle is a string of go-go, get-get, do-do stimulation, crammed with technology, rushing images, and entertainment. By comparison, the Mass is prayerful, thoughtful, and beautifully similar across time and place. As it is meant to be.

The contrast is marked. Compared with what kids see, hear, and do the rest of the week, the Mass looks and sounds out of phase. Where are the graphics and special effects? Who wrote this script? It sounds the same as last week's. Reverence is perceived as slow motion, the uniformity as routine. Thus, not only kids but many adults labor to downshift and contemplate. The slower pace is not one characteristic of their other pursuits.

Some of the craving for an emotional rush eases with age or with having children of one's own. Prayerfully contemplating the liturgy comes more naturally then. Meanwhile, what can you do about your son's worship style?

Keep perspective. The average teen is not in the same spiritual place as his religious parent or parents. Maturing in the Faith, like any kind of maturing, typically takes many years and is marked by slips and slides along the way. How much time and grace did you need to better appreciate the holy? How much time and grace do you still need? Keeping this perspective will calm some of your anxiety over your son's present spiritual bent.

Also, most Mass-going teens believe in God, Christ, and His Church. Their disinterest doesn't necessarily signal a creeping apostasy (or disbelief, for those of you who didn't pay attention in catechism class). It reflects more of an attitude that says, "I'm not getting much out of church right now, so I'm not putting much into it." Of course, the truth is that you get back what you put in.

Apathy borders on disrespect, if it does not equal it. Lack of response reflects lack of respect. Tell your son you expect him to be respectful of God and His house, no matter how he feels about it and no matter whether he wants to or not. He doesn't have to belt out hymns, but he does have to pray with the Mass. Speaking the words is a first step to engagement. The heart may follow in time.

With only twelve years between the oldest and youngest of my ten children, my wife and I have at one time or another sat at Mass with three to six teens. Some of our kids needed only a few lectures about showing respect to God. And others answered me with the same glazed look they wore inside the church.

When mere words didn't elicit cooperation—alas, a standard case with offspring—I set a rule: "Ignore God in His house, and if we go out for breakfast, you watch." For a few weeks, my breakfast bill was pretty light. After that, even the holdouts started to get the idea. Food: a prime mover of the soul. (If we planned to go straight home, I had a whole range of other consequences.)

Am I saying you should discipline for disinterest? Your call. There is nothing psychologically incorrect about curtailing a few perks—if merely post-Mass donuts—because of deliberate indifference. The principle is one of respect. What would you do if your son were rude to you? Are you more deserving of respect than the Father?

# Here, There, and Everywhere

*Dear Dr. Ray,*

*How can I expect my children to be reverent at Mass when I can't stay focused myself?*

*The Drifter*

How can your kids tell you're not focused? You're not playing peekaboo with the lady behind you, are you? Are you counting how many people are wearing shorts? The number of ceiling-fan rotations per minute? Most likely, your drift is internal. Your mind may be meandering, but your body is stationary.

If your roving thoughts were all that noticeable to your kids, you'd hear about it. Besides, your kids are probably not even looking at you. Others are more interesting. "How did that girl's hair get to be that color?"

Do what savvy parents do: Fake it. Your children don't know when your head is elsewhere, so look present. Fold your hands. Kneel straight up; don't rest your bottom on the pew. Practice reverence, and reverence will become your practice.

You and I share the same mental struggle. I begin Mass with an earnest resolve. I'm there to worship, pray, respond, commune.

And I do well, for about the first six minutes. Then I notice a flaw in the wall behind the priest. And my thoughts head to the races: "I never saw that crack before. It wouldn't take much to patch and repaint. I patched a bigger one in the garage last week, and you can hardly tell. But it still needs to be painted. I think I've got some touch-up paint in the basement. I can get to it Saturday before we head up to the game. It's a big one. They're fighting for first place."

In seconds I go from a wall blemish to a pennant race. Other free associations can flow at any time during Mass.

So how does one stay connected at Mass? The first step involves the eyes—specifically, their movement. Resist scanning the congregation (Who is that woman with him?) or trying to pinpoint which kid is causing all the commotion (Why doesn't she deal with her?). Narrow your field of vision. Keep it directed toward the altar area.

The second step also involves the eyes. Close them selectively: during prayers, the Consecration, even the readings. Most sensory input comes through the eyes. Thus, most distractions come through the eyes. Closed eyes suppress distractions.

At the least, you'll look holier. Can you levitate? Make sure to open your eyes before you try.

The other senses aren't so readily controlled. I can't recall too many times when my nose distracted me, except maybe when the kids were really little.

Third step: Open your ears. Therapists practice something called "active listening." It means to pay close attention to what another is saying in order to grasp its real meaning. Actively listen during Mass. What are the words communicating?

Recent changes in some Mass prayers have told me that my listening is often passive, not active, and my responses rote. For example, for nearly five decades, when the priest prayed, "The Lord be with you," I returned, "And also with you." The response is now the more traditional "And with your spirit." Many Masses passed before I finally answered correctly every time. Most humbling was hearing my wife giggle whenever I caught myself and clumsily corrected with something like, "And also with you—your spirit."

Good listening does not come easily or naturally. It takes conscious effort. The Prayer after Communion is a brief, fervent request for the Lord's help to live in thanksgiving for what we've just received. Only when I will myself to listen closely do I hear the prayer's intent.

The temptation is to call attention drift a spiritual weakness. Not necessarily so. Our innate tendency is toward waning attention, especially with something comfortable and familiar, as is the Mass. Someone somewhere once said that good worship does not lie solely in the act of worship but also in the act of pulling oneself back to worshipping.

One more point: You don't have to be the perfect model for everything you teach your kids. If that were so, you'd have little right to teach them much of anything. Human frailty and sin constantly conspire to keep us from the standards we espouse.

The fact that you're not yet the example you want to be—and never will be on this side of eternity—in no way lessens your moral authority. Most of us want our kids to stand morally taller than we do. We don't want to be the upper limit of what they can become.

Drifting focus is unintentional—most of the time, anyway. Regaining focus is intentional. Thus, a conscious move toward the Mass is praiseworthy more than an unconscious move away from it is blameworthy.

Are you paying attention to me?

Part 3

# New Person, Old Past

Coming to Christ for the first time, or growing closer to Him with time, Scripture tells us, creates a new person; the old fades (see 2 Cor. 5:17). Living as a new person will slowly erase the reverberations of one's previous life. But sometimes, direct damage control is necessary. There can be fallout from our past that needs to be repaired.

Even so, it is better to be a new person in faith, conscious of one's struggles and regrets, than to stay the old person, oblivious to what truly matters.

# The Way We Were

*Dear Dr. Ray,*

*Throughout my late teens and twenties, I lived a far-from-moral life. My faith reawakened shortly after the birth of our first child. My three children, all teens now, know a little about my past but none of its ugly details. How much, if anything, do I tell them?*

*Private?*

None of it. End of answer. This book has an editor, however, who says I have to say more. Some questions to guide your decision: Why now? Why to them? What good will it do?

Why now? Is the reason chronological? Meaning, should your kids know more because they're older? Do you know people older than your kids? Have you told them?

My guess is that your parents are older than both you and your kids. Do they know *all* of what you did? Half of it? Okay, 16 percent of it? Do you want to fill them in? You'll probably only make them feel inept as parents or clueless. Save their dignity. Age is not a good rationale for telling someone something he has no need to know.

Complete openness in any relationship is seldom wise. In a spasm of brutal self-disclosure, try telling a relative or friend, "I've never really liked you, and I doubt that you will ever be easy to get along with." Open, honest, not smart. Some remarks are better left unsaid, and some mistakes are better left buried in the past.

Sometimes a relative, often a grandparent, unthinkingly or deliberately pushes you to disclose things. She tells you, within earshot of the kids, "It amazes me that you turned out as good as you did. I was worried there for a while." Or "I don't know why you're so hard on them, especially the way you were at that age." Or she tells your children, "Hey, kids, you ought to ask your dad sometime about his young wild days."

Even when relatives don't enlighten them, as kids get older, they become more savvy social mathematicians. They add up the bits—comments, old photos, jokes, faded tattoos?— to tally that their now morally stable parent was once morally wobbly.

Out of leftover guilt or a belief that total honesty is healthy transparency, you can feel, as the shrinks would say, "a need to share." Don't do it. (Another of my pithy pieces of guidance.)

How much to explain your youth? Speak in generalities; avoid specifics. Reveal lessons learned, but skimp on the who, what, when, where, and how. Acknowledge your old self, but don't make it an afternoon TV talk show.

"Yes, I did things I shouldn't have and wish now I hadn't. For sure, I was younger and dumber. My past is one reason why I'm the parent I am today."

Next question: Why to them? Is there something unique about being your offspring that entitles them to your history? Because they're close blood relatives? Those closest to us often need the most protection from our poorer conduct—present or past.

Are you afraid they'll find out about you someday—where's Grandma?—and you'll have to massage all the gory details? If so, do damage control then. No need to anticipate "what ifs" and answer them before they happen. A line from Colonel Nathan Jessup in *A Few Good Men:* "You have the luxury of not knowing what I know." Let your kids live in luxury.

The foremost question: What good will it do? Ask yourself this any time an unspoken, hard truth is about to be spoken. How will your kids benefit from knowing just how bad you were? Will they relate to you better? "Gee, Mom [Dad], you were once a lot worse than I am now. We have more in common than I thought. I feel the connection, don't you?"

Or will it give them a ready rationale for their misconduct? "You did more as a teenager than I'm doing. See, I'm not that bad."

Will total transparency raise or lower your moral authority? Will you hear, "I never realized how much you've changed from the way you were, Father. You have so much to teach me"? Or will you hear, "How can you tell me what's right or wrong when you lived the way you did? It was all right for you, but it's not all right for me?"

Whenever a parent watches his kids repeat his old ways, he can feel the urge to correct them by sharing his past. More often than not, that doesn't work so well. Kids are prone to interpret your past as a rationale for their present. If someone—young or old—really wants to do something, he searches hard for a justification. Don't be that justification.

So what, if anything, do you tell? Once more, be general. Focus on why you now are who you are. Your parenting has roots in your past experience. You know personally what can happen when a child maneuvers around a parent's guidance. In short, your past helped shape your present.

Most kids are not of the age or maturity to benefit from their parents' misspent youth. There are better ways for them to learn.

# So Did You

*Dear Dr. Ray,*

*How do I respond to an adolescent boy who, upon having social limits put on him, accuses, "You did worse when you were my age."*

*Dumber Then*

Well, did you? If so, whatever he knows about it, don't give him more grist. (See the previous question and response.) Your past, however wrong or stupid, is not his concern unless you wish it to be. Remember, though, what you say can and will be held against you.

Now let's answer your son. First and foremost, your moral authority as a parent does not depend one whit upon your moral conduct as a teen. The process of maturing implies that we are more foolish and shortsighted when younger. However you wish to impart this truth to your son, do so. Don't expect him to understand or agree. That's part of his immaturity. Nevertheless, you are, in essence, saying, "Childhood illogic will not weaken my resolve as a parent or cripple me with guilt."

Admit to your son an indisputable fact: You were once a child. "You're right, I did teenager things when I was a teenager." Again though, you don't have to reveal all or feel obliged to respond to each of his probing questions. He's likely not so much interested in your youth as in getting ammunition for his.

Contrary to what your son thinks, you are not so old as to recall only in a misty haze what impulses, desires, and dangers accompany youth. It is your memory of once being his age that makes you acutely aware of how to help him safely travel similar roads. Part of being a good parent is remembering being bad as a kid.

Your masterstroke: Tell your son he is very lucky that you once did wrong and bad things. Through your own misconduct, you realize the wisdom in protecting him from his own mistakes. Whatever you might once have gotten away with was not to your benefit.

Relevant here is the adage "A foolish person doesn't learn from his mistakes; a smart person learns from his mistakes; a really smart person learns from the mistakes of others."

You could say to your son, "You're right. I did do worse than you when I was your age. And so I want to raise someone who's a lot better than I was. And I think that's happening."

Not much bugs a teen more than a parent who compliments as she disciplines.

# Conversion Guilt

*Dear Dr. Ray,*

*I returned to the Church two years ago, at age forty-three. Until then, I raised my children (now ages sixteen and twelve) with Christmas-and-Easter religion. I've got lots of guilt over the lost years. And my kids have been slow to accept a deeper faith for themselves.*

*Too-Late-Smart Mom*

Thanks be to God, He opened your eyes. While He transformed your life later than you'd like, it is not too late. A late conversion is infinitely better than no conversion.

Of course, had you stayed as you were, you wouldn't be nagged by regrets. You might have ignored the God-sized holes in your life and your children's lives, for a while anyway. But awareness is almost always better than ignorance. It is better to feel bad over what you missed than never to know what you missed.

Does this mean you should live with guilt over lost opportunity? No. It means, live grateful for your knowledge. Gratitude will trump guilt. It's hard to feel guilty when you're grateful. Guilt is stoked by self-blame: Why didn't I see the light sooner? Why did

I chase wrong things? Why should my children have to suffer for my blind spots? Is it too late?

Answer emotion with reason. Not all who come to Christ come young. Some of the holiest saints found God in adulthood. All the apostles were called as grown-ups. God's plans are a mystery. He must want you where you are now. Don't question His timing.

Conversion brings forgiveness. God pardons what you did or didn't do as a mom. Though you followed your rules, not His, you didn't yet realize that. You loved your children as you knew, though you didn't know what you now know. God is not holding your "failures" against you. Will you reject His mercy? Will you debate God's wisdom?

A priest told me that moving closer to Christ is like moving closer to a bright light. As we near, we notice flaws in ourselves that we never before saw. In your earlier motherhood, you lived by your own light. Then you came closer to the real Light. Now, not only can you see more clearly, but the light shines on anyone you are holding by the hand.

Your kids may want their old mom back. She gave them more freedoms. She thought more as their friends' parents do; she followed cultural trends. This new mom is making some course changes. She's raising her moral bar, tightening some rules. Who is this woman, anyway? Who has taken over her body? Indeed, who?

Their objections aside, the kids, in time, will notice that this new mom is a better mom. She's more caring, affectionate, and giving. Her discipline is softer, with less scolding and volume. The kids feel the positives. As they age, they'll feel those positives more durably.

Understandably, your children have been slow to accept a deeper faith. You willingly chose to change; they may not be quite there yet. Be patient.

Patience, however, doesn't mean "This is their decision. I won't try to influence them." Certainly influence them. Live the Faith: Attend Mass together, pray before meals, bless them at bedtime, read the Bible, sign them up for CCD, find charitable activities for all, educate on morals and virtue. Give them what you found.

While your children don't see this through forty-three-year-old eyes, they've gotten an earlier start than you. Their ages total twenty-eight, still fifteen years shy of your age at rebirth.

# New Old Wife

*Dear Dr. Ray,*

*My husband and I have been married thirteen years – no children. For most of that time, we were both nonpracticing Catholics. In the last three years, I've had a strong awakening of my faith, and my husband is not so happy with the new me. He says I'm not the same woman he married.*

*Remade*

He is right. You are not the same woman he married. You're a better one.

The rule rather than the exception: No two spouses are on an identical spiritual page. Some aren't even in the same book. One has memorized the daily Confession times at all parishes within a twenty-five-mile radius; the other struggles to stay awake during a six-minute Sunday homily. One prays the Rosary in Aramaic while levitating; the other needs a teleprompter to say a complete Glory Be.

Sometimes the roles shift. Raised solidly Catholic, I took the lead Church-wise upon meeting my wife, Randi, who grew up with little formal religion. So I appeared the more "religious" one.

A few years into our marriage, Randi turned more strongly to Christianity and ultimately to Catholicism. I'd like to believe my holy example influenced her, but she maintains that were it not for me, she would have converted sooner.

My wife's conversion was fervent and continues to be so. Anyone paying attention will see that she is the more religious one. In my defense, I no longer need a teleprompter, even for the Apostles' Creed.

Whatever the spiritual distance between you and your husband, don't let it cause strife. Without weakening your internal God presence, you can modify your expression of it.

If you attend weekday Mass, don't always go when Hubby is home. Work your Mass schedule around his work schedule and his other times away. Arrange church activities to compete least with marriage activities. Don't fill most of your free time with parish functions, including protracted phone calls with new, like-minded church friends.

Preset one, not every, Christian station on your car radio. When driving together, listen to your husband's stations. I know, you couldn't care less about the benefits of the designated hitter in baseball. But for now, this may be where his mind plays.

Is your husband bothered by your tuning out his, and once your, favorite TV programs? Without compromising your morals, find things to watch together—football, World War II chronicles, *Modern Tank Repair*, *Gator Guys*—the stuff wives record to watch again and again.

Our Lord teaches, "But when you pray, go into your room and shut the door and pray to your Father who is in secret" (Matt. 6:6). Lower the profile of your prayer time and spiritual reading. And for sure, don't speak to your husband in Latin.

Your husband may not so much be threatened by your new life; he may fear that your old life with him is passing. As he feels left out of your world, he may resent your world. Find ways to enter his. Read up on the designated-hitter pros and cons. Ask him if it's smart to call a draw play on third down and twelve.

You're not denying Christ or His Church. Nor are you hiding your light under a basket. You are not weakening your connection to God; you are strengthening your connection with your spouse.

One change that's hard but has the most potential to change your husband: Show him how much the new you benefits him. Show him that his post-conversion wife is a better spouse than his pre-conversion one — more agreeable, more giving, more affectionate, just easier to live with. I know, it's a whole lot simpler to pray alone in the car than to improve one's personality. Changing oneself, however, is the best way to change another.

Are you already the sweeter spouse? If so, are you at your holiness limit? Did you rise there in just three years? That's fast. The paradox of faithful living: The more you mature, the more you have room to mature.

What if your husband takes advantage of his more saintly wife? She is more compromising, so he becomes less compromising. She is more pleasant, so he is less pleasant. This is unlikely. Most people react positively to better treatment; very few react negatively. Your spouse may not be all that religious, but he's probably not all that unreasonable. When someone's behavior makes another's life better, the other person almost always welcomes it.

How long until your more loving wifehood converts your husband's attitude? I have no idea. (Did you spend your own money on this book?) But I do know that however long it takes, you will be moving in a better direction than currently.

Through it all, your motive to be a better spouse is stronger than his: Your faith tells you to be one.

# New but Not Improved

*The more I try to live my faith, the less I like who I am. I think I had a better self-image pre-Christian.*

It may seem so. But upon whose judgment was your self-image based? Yours or God's?

Thinking well of oneself is psychologically pretty easy: Avoid honest self-scrutiny. Don't look too far inward for the stuff of human frailty.

Once upon a time, you were the judge of your virtue. You set the standards, so how could you not be satisfied with yourself? A natural inclination is to lower one's personal moral bar to meet one's overall conduct. It's a defense in service of the ego.

Because you now desire to live more for God and less for yourself, it's understandable to experience some feelings of falling short. The more you peer within, the more you see where and how you're not following Christ. From the seemingly sluggish pace of your spiritual growth springs the self-critique.

One other fellow talked of this same frustration long ago. His name was Paul. "I do not understand my own actions. For I do not do what I want, but I do the very thing I hate" (Rom. 7:15). Your self-image struggle can create what psychologists call "cognitive dissonance." It is holding two contradictory ideas in one's head at the same time. One idea is that you believe you can rest in the peace Christ promises His followers. The other is that you feel less than peaceful about your efforts to be a follower.

To keep your peace, believe Christ's. His love is unconditional. It doesn't ebb and flow with your moral successes and failures. God values you infinitely, and He knows your frailty far better than you know it.

God asks for your effort. To paraphrase C. S. Lewis: God wants people of a certain kind.[1] He doesn't scrutinize our ledger of goods and bads and then decide whether He likes us. He wants people who relentlessly reach toward Him, despite their falls. The most reliable sign of our love for God lies in our perseverance past our moral stumbles and fumbles. And He gives us the strength to persevere.

Suppose, though, that you start to feel comfortable with faithfulness. If you have to say so yourself, you're getting to be a pretty holy human. Could this sense of spiritual self-esteem mean spiritual pride?

Certainly, one wants to take contentment in faithful obedience. Just as certainly, one doesn't want to get too self-satisfied. In that direction lurks pride, and pride is a falsely inflated self-image.

Your current self-image may be fueled by feelings. You don't *feel* good about your faith walk. Because of your moral ups and downs,

---

[1] "We might think that God wanted simply obedience to a set of rules: whereas He really wants people of a particular sort." C. S. Lewis, *Mere Christianity* (New York: Macmillan, 1943), 77.

you *feel* inadequate. Because of your failures, you *feel* unworthy. As elsewhere emphasized, feelings are a fickle guide to truth. Because you feel something doesn't make it so. Good thinking has to over-rule undeserved bad feelings.

Good thinking begins with recognizing reality. And the reality is that you are a better person now than you were pre-Christian. You are living by higher standards. You are more self-aware. And it is better to be more self-aware, even if that means a clear view of one's shortcomings, than to be self-satisfied. Self-satisfaction stunts personal growth. It keeps one from getting closer to God.

What you are is a child of God, one nearer to Him than you once were. His bright light shows more of your flaws, but it also gives warmth and healing. All in all, a really good trade-off, one to your benefit.

Part 4

# Counter Catholic

Bishop Fulton Sheen, a highly respected teacher of the Faith in the 1950s and 1960s, observed, "There are not a hundred people in America who hate the Catholic Church. There are millions of people who hate what they wrongly believe to be the Catholic Church—which is, of course, quite a different thing."[2]

Not to quibble with someone as wise and holy as Bishop Sheen, but it seems many people these days denounce the Catholic Church exactly for who she is.

Wrongheaded critiques don't only create religious distance between people. They also create relationship distance. Knowing how and when to answer people who question the Faith is a giant step—if not toward reconciliation, then toward personal peace.

[2] Fulton Sheen, *Radio Replies: Classic Answers to Timeless Questions about the Catholic Faith* (El Cajon, CA: Catholic Answers, 2014), introduction.

# Misguided Missionary

*Dear Dr. Ray,*

*My eight-year-old daughter plays with a neighbor girl, age ten. Lately, her friend, who is not Catholic, has been talking down our Catholic Faith. This bothers my daughter, but she doesn't want to lose her friend.*

*Neighborly Advice?*

I've not met one ten-year-old who collects anti-Catholic tracts or who's written a theological treatise on the differing Christian traditions. If, by chance, she's one, ask to see her research—before the next play date.

If she's a typical ten-year-old, what she is saying is a rephrase of what she is hearing. She is parroting some big people, at home or elsewhere. On her own, she probably hasn't formed too many anti-Catholic sentiments yet.

Since you don't know exactly who is putting these words into her mind, your first step would be toward her house, specifically toward her parents. Describe for them what is happening, using a few concrete examples. Avoid accusations or recriminations. You come in peace. Your mission is a fact-finding one.

Your neighbors may be totally unaware of their daughter's actions. They could be embarrassed. If so, you won't have to say or do much more. They will rein her in. Problem solved. Little friends back to playing together in ecumenical harmony.

On the other hand, they could be pleased that their daughter is learning so young to evangelize. Again charitably, tell them you'd like to correct any of their daughter's misunderstandings, for both girls' sakes. If they're open, you'd also be willing to clear up any of their own misunderstandings about the Catholic Church.

Should they accept your offer, they'll show themselves inclined to better understanding. Should they reject it, becoming upset at your "counter-evangelizing," they may move to protect their child from you and yours. Much will hinge upon how deep-rooted their misconceptions are.

Defensiveness sometimes subsides when the emotions around it do. Perhaps later, your neighbors will settle, rethink the matter, and respect your wishes, allowing the girls to return to uncomplicated friendship. Time and more play visits will tell.

Of course, your daughter may not tell you everything, as she wishes to protect a friendship. Therefore, watch for signs that something is bothering her: a sober mood, vague remarks ("I just wish she'd be nicer"), atypical behavior (retreating to her bedroom), questions such as, "Mom, why do we pray to Mary?" You sense your daughter is upset even when she's keeping it inside.

Suppose the friend's critiques keep coming. Use them to educate, and it will strengthen your daughter's faith—and yours too. If the critiques are more unsettling to her than your words are comforting, you may have to limit the friendship or, at a minimum, keep it within your earshot. Your neighbor girl is not a bad influence; her wrongheaded religious prejudices are.

Will your daughter agree with your decision? Probably not. The best of parents are routinely misunderstood—in the short-term, not in the long-term.

# Youth Think

*Dear Dr. Ray,*

*My fifteen-year-old daughter has been attending a youth group at her friend's non-Catholic church. It offers social activities and lectures by the pastor. I'm a little nervous about what she could hear about her Catholic Faith.*

*Wary*

I wouldn't be nervous, as long as what she's hearing is the truth. Otherwise, I would be nervous.

Non-Catholic churches have long offered youth groups. Some of them are Catholic-charitable, some are Catholic-tolerant, and some are Catholic-hostile. Which is your daughter attending?

You could ask her what she is hearing. Her report, however, might not be completely reliable. For one, she may not be aware of which of her Catholic beliefs are being questioned, especially if it's subtle. For another, her group good times may color the picture she gives to you.

You could accompany her a few times. (Gasp! Make sure you walk in twenty minutes later, sit back by the door, and sport a fake mustache.) Talk with the group leaders and the pastor. What's their understanding of Catholicism? What do they know? Listen to a selection of the pastor's sermons, in person or recorded. Read the church's mission statement or a sampling of its literature.

Talk with the mother of your daughter's friend or other church members you might know. Adult attitudes tend to trickle down to the youth. Even if the pastor considers Catholics fellow Christians, some of the congregation might not. Their kids could see it as their Christian duty to pull the new kid out of her "false religion."

How well does your daughter know her Catholic Faith? Can she express it? Defend it? Can she discern a sincere question from a veiled challenge? Or explain a Bible quote that seems to contradict Catholic teaching?

There are teens who are well-spoken missionaries for the Church—for their age. But the most mature teen is still a teen. Faith tempered by fire involves years of experience and truth seeking. Most adolescents are pulled by the social side of youth groups and pay minimal heed to the doctrinal side.

Should all your initial reservations be soothed, remain vigilant. Keep an ongoing dialogue with your daughter. Make it easy for her to bring any questions or confusion to you. The truth has nothing to fear from the false.

Eventually, you may conclude you can't completely counter the pull of your daughter's friend's religion. Over her objections, you may have to end her attendance.

An option: Good Catholic youth groups are out there. Check with area churches. There's likely one close by.

# Higher Reeducation

*Dear Dr. Ray,*

*Our nineteen-year-old son returned home from college this summer full of questions and objections about the Catholic Faith. Now he seems to feel obligated to correct his fifteen-year-old brother's thinking.*

*In the Middle*

The reigning academic mindset feels obligated to correct, attack even, the thinking of traditionally religious students. Having a child's faith dogmatically assaulted is bad enough; it's worse to pay someone to do it. Unfortunately, Christian parents in large numbers are unaware of what all is included in a college education these days.

Your son's enlightened thinking is shedding some light on your thinking, specifically about his ongoing education. You may have to rethink: Is he in the best place for majoring in wisdom?

Given that your son is bringing his "enlightenment" home, your first assignment: Let's college-proof younger brother. Rein in older brother. Absolutely no reeducating his sibling.

Invite older brother instead to lay all his newfound knowledge on you or your spouse. What exactly is he being told and by whom?

What are the backgrounds and motives of these sources? What is their history? Many objections to religion are based not on reason but on opinion. Most likely, the arguments that your son finds so intellectually heavy rest on sand. But he doesn't know enough to know that.

As always, it's smart to know, or at least find out, how to answer well. If you flounder, you could further convince him that his professors and fellow students are indeed smarter about the Catholic Church than you are.

Novel revelations, however wrongheaded, can drive someone toward a false intellectual superiority. This is happening if your son argues bothersome little basics like facts and logic. He's defending his turf, being pushed more by a need to be right than a desire to think right. Arrogance often accompanies nascent knowledge.

What if college brother uses stealth to reeducate younger brother? You will then have to act. Consequences will follow: loss of car, computer, cell phone, social freedoms, money. Though he is nineteen, you still have plenty of leverage.

Your son could accuse you of stifling free speech and academic discourse. So be it. Freedom of speech has limits. He doesn't need to push his religious reformation upon every family member.

Talk with little brother. What has big brother told him? What are his questions about it? What has most bothered him?

Give little brother the Church's solid answers to the antagonistic questions thrown at her. The Church has heard it all and has been answering challenges since the time of Christ. Your son has nothing to fear from the secular dogmas of "really smart" people.

Enroll your younger son in your prerequisite course in religious instruction. You'll be preparing him for college.

# Bible Versed

*Dear Dr. Ray,*

*I've been attending a women's Bible study at a nondenominational church. I enjoy it and am learning, but some of my Catholic beliefs are being disputed by their quoting Scripture.*

*Lone Voice*

Contrary to popular misunderstanding, the Church has always encouraged knowledge of Scripture. That's why every Sunday Mass has three Bible readings, which cover much of the Old and New Testaments every three years. Formal Bible studies, until relatively recently, have been the mainstay of other Christian groups, as Catholics have traditionally looked toward the Church to teach the Faith as well as accurately interpret Scripture. Now Catholic studies are fast on the rise.

Many non-Catholic Bible studies emphasize two basics. One, Jesus is Lord; with that, Catholics fully agree. And two, the Catholic Church is wrong or, worse, evil, as she is leading countless people away from true Christianity.

The Catholic Church is the largest religious body in the United States, with some seventy-plus million baptized. Sadly, those who accept her whole teaching, or even simply attend Sunday Mass, total a much smaller number. It is said that the second largest religious group in the United States consists of fallen-away Catholics, those heading toward either other churches or a spiritual vacuum.

Predicting by the numbers alone, one or more of your study's members once were Catholic and carry a raft of misunderstandings or resentments about their former religion. Further, their ire is often grounded in personal experience, giving them credibility with the study's non-Catholics.

In my thirties, I drifted from the Church and began to attend several non-Catholic studies. While I met many sincere, God-seeking Christians, I also met anti-Catholic bias—some from ignorance, some from arrogance. In one study, a former Catholic declared with a tone of leftover bitterness, "I was raised Catholic and went to Mass for over twenty years, and I never heard Jesus Christ proclaimed 'Lord and Savior.'"

Out of curiosity, I obtained a missalette from the previous week's Mass and counted how many times Jesus was called Lord, Savior, Lamb of God, Son of God, God. Total: thirty-six. This did not include any of His titles that the priest used in his homily. I wondered if I should ask my friend, "Where were you all those years?"

Admittedly, people's arguments at times did stir up doubts for me. Though I knew the basics of what the Church taught, I didn't know the reasons, from Scripture or history. What if these other Christians were right and the Church was wrong? I mean, they had Bible verses to buttress their case.

Thank God for my confusion. It pushed me to seek answers, not from ex- or anti-Catholics but from the Church herself. Obviously, she was no stranger to these objections, having heard and dispelled them for centuries—many of them from the time of Christ.

So I read, studied, listened—and found the Church's teachings to make complete sense and to reflect what Christians have historically believed. My search led me back to the Church I knew as a child.

How confident and comfortable are you in answering the misunderstandings you hear? Do you know not only the whats of your Faith but the whys? You needn't be a Scripture scholar or a theologian to speak. A well-informed Catholic can well inform anyone willing to listen.

The operative adjective is "well-informed." Trying to fumble one's way through an explanation only further convinces people that Catholics don't know much about their Faith. As the saying warns, better to stay silent and appear dumb than to open one's mouth and remove all doubt.

As I learned to better explain Church teaching, some of those in my former Bible study were intrigued by what they heard, so much so that they began their own search, which led to conversion. Educate yourself to educate others.

And find a good Catholic Bible study. They are out there—more all the time.

# Conversion Critiques

*Dear Dr. Ray,*

*My parents raised me in a faithful non-Catholic Christian household. They are still upset over my Catholic conversion four years after marrying my Catholic husband. Mostly they avoid the topic, but every so often, they demean some Church teaching or practice.*

*Relatively Hurt*

You use the word "demean." So I'm assuming that the content or tone of your parents' remarks is hostile to the Church and hurtful to you. Honest questions beget honest answers. Critiques often convey that no answers, no matter how gentle and logical, will satisfy.

You must wonder, "Why are they still upset four years later?" Are they taking your conversion personally? Not only did you abandon the religion of your youth, but you abandoned the religion they invested so much of themselves in teaching you. As they see it, you rejected not only their faith but them too.

When time and opportunity permit, reassure your parents of your gratitude for the foundation they gave you. Now you are building upon that foundation. Something tells me you've already done this, but I do need to fill out my answer.

Explain to your folks—to the degree you can—that your journey to the Catholic Church is not a repudiation of their beliefs. Rather, your desire is to follow where Christ leads and to worship as a family with your husband (and children).

Ask your parents, "What is a Christian? What are your basics for following Christ?" You will likely be able to agree with most, perhaps all, of them. Your message is: I have not left Christianity. I have found it in greater fullness.

Do your mother and father think your husband or his family pressured you to convert? It wasn't your idea, but theirs? What's more, was their pressure subtle, below your awareness? Even as you tell them that wasn't so, be ready to receive a response like, "Well, you may not see it, but in fact ..."

You can only articulate your true reasons. What they choose to accept is beyond your control. Of course, the better you know the Faith, the better you can explain your reasons.

When the questions and criticisms come, have a restrained, ever-ready reply: "Mom, do you want to know why the Church teaches that?" Or "I can give you an answer if you want one, Dad." Then observe their demeanor. It should reveal to you why they are judging as they are.

What if your parents aren't the least bit interested in knowing anything more about the Catholic Faith? What if they are convinced of their truth, not wishing to hear any other?

Do not argue, dispute, or get into a religious tit for tat. To win them, your ally is the Fourth Commandment: Honor thy father and mother. "Honor" does not mean you have to concur with their every thought or obey their every wish. It means you will give them their due respect and act to keep friction to a minimum, especially friction based on religion.

As they see that being Catholic is making you a better daughter, wife, and mother, will they be more open to giving your religion some credibility? Many people are not convinced by better arguments. They are, however, moved by better treatment.

# Sins against Society

*Dear Dr. Ray,*

*I'm a mother of five children and happily pregnant with my sixth. I'm amazed at how free people feel to disparage my family size. I'm reluctant to tell anyone I'm expecting again.*

*Getting Quieter*

Tolerance is the pervasive, preeminent new moral virtue. Whatever others want to do is their choice—indeed, their right—and is to be accepted, even celebrated. Yet our society is quite narrow in its tolerance. For all its vaunted openness, the tolerance movement is riddled with ironies.

Irony #1: *Tolerance for all, except some.* Not everyone deserves to think his or her own way. Tolerance is reserved for those who think the right way, as defined by reigning secular rules. The largest group of "non-acceptables" are traditional values, especially those of the Christian faith and especially the Catholic Faith.

Irony #2: *Tolerance redefines itself, moving with cultural winds.* One moral edict that nowadays must be accepted is sexual freedom—except, as you hear firsthand, the sexual freedom to have babies in marriage.

A quote attributed to G. K. Chesterton is "When people stop believing in God, the danger is not that they believe in nothing, the danger is that they'll believe in anything." In God's absence, or at least His lower profile, society gets to define what constitutes a "sin." Three current ones are: smoking, spanking, and having more than 1.78 children.

Irony #3: *Sacrifice is called selfishness.* Mothers and fathers who accept children as God's gifts, who daily give of themselves for their larger than "normal" family, and who live with fewer material comforts are accused of being selfish or of "breeding" in order to meet some underlying psychological needs. Wanting children is greedy. Tell that to these parents' checkbooks.

Irony #4: *Plenty is no longer enough.* No society in human history has enjoyed our level of resources and abundance. Yet a standard objection against having several children is material: "How can you take care of them?" Meaning what? Food? Shelter? Education? Cars? Bathrooms? Bedrooms?

A generation or two ago, the typical family home was around a thousand square feet. One bathroom, two or more kids per bedroom, no air conditioning, one phone, and a single-car garage. Parents who successfully raised families in such deprived conditions now wonder how their grown children can maintain a favorable family lifestyle in a house twice or more times as large, with multiple everything. One child per bedroom is now the upper limit.

During our adoption screening for our fourth child, the social worker asked my wife and me, "Do you have enough bedrooms?" I was tempted to answer, "Well, they have walls, beds, and carpet, but no TVs." But Randi shot me a "don't go there" look. At the time, we had three bedrooms, which seemed quite sufficient to me. As a fallback, Randi and I could move to the couch. Well, maybe I could.

When my oldest daughter, Hannah, entered college, the school's president spoke about the freshman adjustment to having a room-mate. At which Hannah exclaimed, "Only one?" She had entered dormitory heaven.

Irony #5: *Okay for me, not for you.* Too-many-kids reactions regularly come from those who had large families themselves—grandparents and others of their generation who routinely had four-plus children. Nevertheless, they question why their offspring would want more offspring.

Irony #6: *People of faith also question.* It is understandable that the nonreligious would look askance at parents who challenge the childbearing allowance numerically; their perspective is slanted by society's. One would expect those of faith to better understand the God-ordained gift of children. Sadly, many now observe family life through a lens more secular than faith-lit.

Irony #7: *One mustn't criticize others—except mothers.* Those who religiously shun talking politics or religion feel unrestrained license to opine about the most personal of someone's life decisions. The cliches are predictably similar—thought clever but, in fact, tiresome. "Are they all yours?" "Don't you have a TV?" "So this is it, right?" (This last question sometimes follows child number two, almost always coming after child number three.) "You've got your boy and girl [the "complete" family], so are you finished?"

Sometimes the intrusions come with an edge: "I hope you're not thinking of more?" "How can you give each the attention it needs?" (The pronoun itself is instructive.) "What about college?" (The financial often lurks.)

Verbally cornering veteran mothers is not without risk. After all, these are women uncowed by years of living in close proximity to multiple little human beings. A rude remark or two can be swatted away as effortlessly as a seven-year-old's tattle.

"Is this all your family?" "Of course not; our oldest is at home with the triplets."

"Haven't you ever heard of birth control?" "Yes, I've heard of it. Why?"

"Do you know what causes this?" "No, please tell me."

"Is your husband going to get fixed?" "I don't think he's broken."

"Are you going to have more?" "Well, not right this minute."

"Don't you think you have too many children?" "Which one should I give back?"

"I'm glad it's you and not me." "I think my kids are glad too." Ouch!

Sometimes the concerns are for Mom: "I just worry about you." "Be careful you don't overload yourself." "How's your stress level?" "Can you manage it all?" "Are you doing okay?"

Even when well-meaning, these questions imply that Mother doesn't quite understand what she's doing to herself. Isn't she sacrificing herself for all these children? Well, yes, she is. That is exactly her intent.

It's good to answer sour with sweet: "A soft answer turns away wrath" (Prov. 15:1). "We've always been grateful for our kids." "We want whomever God gives us."

Sometimes a good response is no response—a smile, a shrug, a lost look. Lost looks silently say, "I don't understand your point." What else can anyone expect from someone who has deliberately fried her brain circuitry with so many offspring?

In the end, what wins over naysayers most is the children themselves. Parents of plenty typically invest themselves plenty in their families. In time, others see that your children are not emotionally and materially shortchanged. Rather, they are maturing into individuals admired by those who once didn't understand you.

Part 5

# Faithful Distress

Faith brings beyond-this-world peace. Our Lord is definite about that. How, then, can it also bring distress? Simple answer: It can't. It is not one's faith that brings turmoil; it is misunderstandings about the Faith.

If our love for Christ fosters self-reproach, we have to look not at Christ but at ourselves. The question is not "What is it about Christianity that is making me feel bad?" The question is "What am I doing—or thinking—to make me feel bad?"

# A Piece of Peace

*Dear Dr. Ray,*

*I know my faith should be a source of peace. But I don't always feel that peace. I worry about sinning, and even after Confession, I don't always feel forgiven.*

*Praying for Peace*

Anytime anyone is passionately moved about anything, going to a self-sabotaging extreme is a temptation. Faith is meant to be taken to an extreme—a self-renewing one, not a self-defeating one.

God calls us to have a healthy sensitivity to the sickness of sin. The closer you move toward God, the more you know how ugly sin is. In no way does this mean that you won't sin again, regularly. It means you don't want to sin. It means your repentance—your desire not to sin next time—grows stronger. The saying is: the difference between a saint and a sinner is that the saint gets up one more time than he falls.

You say you "worry about sinning." Someone who deliberately sins doesn't worry about it. Your worry is one sign that you hate sin. Your lack of peace comes from taking your worry too far.

All through life, we are at war with our human weakness. And we have some elite company. Read St. Paul's Letter to the Romans, chapter 7: "I do not understand my own actions. For I do not do what I want, but I do the very thing I hate." He laments his condition but rests in the cure: "Thanks be to God [it is] through Jesus Christ our Lord" (vv. 15, 25).

You have sentiments in common with Paul—up to a point. He, too, sees himself as a sinner, but he also trusts in God's pardon. He sees that he falls because of his human frailty, but he trusts that God is ever ready to pick him up.

You use the same word to describe how you perceive both your lack of peace and your uncertainty about God's mercy: *feel*. In the mindset of our hyper-psychologizing culture, feelings supposedly reveal the genuine self. One can't dispute feelings without disputing oneself. Feelings rule.

This mindset directly clashes with the Christian mindset. Yes, feelings are ingrained in who we are, but they answer to our "image of God" qualities—intellect and will.

You say you don't *feel* peace or forgiveness. But do your feelings reflect what is? In fact, are you not in God's peace, and, in fact, are you not forgiven? Feelings can't negate God's promises. He promises that an honest confession brings forgiveness—period. What one feels afterward is irrelevant.

> Return, O faithless sons,
> I will heal your faithlessness. (Jer. 3:22)

What underlies your lack of peace? Guilt over having sinned? Not measuring up to self-imposed saintly standards? Concern that your actions belie your intentions? Not one of these, nor all taken together, trumps God's pledge: You are forgiven, no matter what your feelings tell you. What you know must overrule what you feel. Feelings can be the great deceivers.

Christ has said repeatedly—for those of us hard of spiritual hearing—that He wants to forgive. He told Peter that he must forgive "not ... seven times, but seventy times seven" (Matt. 18:22). That is biblical language for "completely and continuously." If our Lord wants you to forgive others fully, does this advice not apply to forgiving yourself? Or to His forgiving you? Does Christ ignore His own teachings?

Cognitive dissonance may be working here. This comes from holding two opposing thoughts in one's head simultaneously. The clash creates dissonance, a sense of tension or, in your words, a lack of peace. For you, one thought is: I am a Christian, and God loves me. Its antagonist: How can I keep sinning and expect God to keep absolving me?

Because that's who God is. He doesn't have to force Himself to be merciful. There is no limit to His occasions of forgiveness (seventy-one times seven?). His being is mercy.

If you willfully, deliberately embrace sin, then a disturbed peace is warranted. Conscience is making its presence felt. If, however, you sin out of human weakness, then whatever guilt remains post repentance is not from God. It comes from a misunderstanding of God's ways—or maybe from the devil, "who accuses [us] day and night," even "before our God" (Rev. 12:10).

Peace endures when knowledge and emotions coincide. I feel peace because I know God forgives me. If the head and heart are at odds, however, the head must exert itself. It will bring wayward feelings into line.

Peace comes from believing God, not from believing one's feelings.

# More Faith, Less Depression?

*Dear Dr. Ray,*

*I'm fifty-three years old and have struggled on and off throughout my life with depression. Since my return to the Church twelve years ago, I've felt that if I had more trust in God, I'd have less depression.*

*Better by Now?*

Depression has myriad causes. Without knowing your history, I can't know what underlies your depression. I do, however, know people with similar doubts about faith and depression.

Some depression is chemical. It reflects dysfunctional brain pathways. What these pathways are, medical science is just beginning to unravel. Other depression follows crushing life events—the death of a loved one, a fractured marriage, illness, financial calamity, trauma.

Most depressions are born and raised by the way one interprets everyday stresses and strains. Identical circumstances can bury one person in despair and temporarily ruffle another, depending upon the meaning given them.

When the depression is biochemically driven, faith doubts are unfounded. Proper medication—which the Church supports—often raises the mood, which then lowers the self-reproach. With most depression, talk therapy helps, as it aims to uncover and correct whatever "misthinking" is fueling the melancholy.

Your misthinking is that your depression is a sign of your weak Christianity. Your thought equation is: Less faith equals more depression. This can carry some truth if questions of religion rattle your moods or if you are scrupulously tormented by your "sinfulness." Otherwise, depression typically comes from a mix of factors, with one's faith walk a smaller one.

If your faith equals that of God's holiest saints, you can find peace even in the middle of emotional downs. As St. Paul writes, "For I have learned, in whatever state I am, to be content" (Phil. 4:11). If you're anything like me, however, or almost all of Christ's followers, your faith is a work in progress: It won't be complete until you see Him face-to-face. Until that day, you live in an imperfect state of trust.

"If you have faith as a grain of mustard seed, you will say to this mountain, 'Move from hence to yonder place,' and it will move" (Matt. 17:20). Given that, my faith would have to multiply many times over just to rival a mustard seed. Not that more trust in God's providence won't lighten my mood. It will. The error comes in thinking the converse—that is, incomplete faith darkens one's mood.

More faith can change a person's self-view. Depression is routinely wrapped around a poor self-image. "I feel insignificant, worthless even." The experts intone that to ease depression, one needs to think well of himself, to believe he is a worthwhile person. The catch is that the person trying to uplift herself is also the one plagued by self-doubt.

If Ray Guarendi declares himself to be special, how much weight does my vote carry? How much credibility do I have to testify to my own specialness? (Though, as a shrink, I suppose I could administer some tests to myself.)

On the other hand, if the Creator of the universe has declared me of infinite worth — as He has — the testimony is indisputable. It's true self-esteem. Accepting God's view of you will dignify *your* view of you. With that will come greater peace.

Depression can be marked by feelings of being unlovable. "I don't love me much, so I can't see how others could either." If God, the source of all love, pronounces me lovable — as He does — who am I to question Him? Am I more psychologically attuned to me than He is? Trusting God's judgment above mine results in a better mood.

Suppose I grapple with doubts about my competence — as a spouse, a parent, a Christian. Others look so much more capable than I. By comparison, I think I constantly fall short.

God doesn't grade on a curve. He is not about to fail me because I'm not in the upper 30 percent of child-raising skill, spousal appeal, or Christian saintliness. My achievements or competence have little — sometimes nothing — to do with my connection to God. If God scored on results, we'd all fall short. I'd have to enroll in an ongoing remedial life course.

Our shortcomings can spur us to reach higher for God. The "people of a certain kind" that God wants are those who continue to seek Him, whatever their strengths and weaknesses.

Faith is an infinite well of emotional strength. With God's help, it will deepen until the day we leave this world for the next. In the meanwhile, to chastise yourself for insufficient faith leading to depression is to misunderstand what faith is. It also misunderstands what depression is.

# No Time Like the Future

*Dear Dr. Ray,*

*My son is thirty years old. He left the Church shortly after college and has never returned. I pray for him constantly, but I'm getting discouraged because nothing is changing.*

*Wearying*

It's better said: Nothing is changing that you can see. Something might well be changing that you can't see. The heart often moves some distance before conduct follows.

Talking metaphysically—I do have a fancy degree, you know—relevant here is the very essence of time. Time is a measurement of change. Because we humans are time-bound, everything we experience is always passing. In your case, eight years seems like a long time, looking forward, anyway, and not backward.

God is not time-bound. He exists outside of time. Whether something takes five minutes or five millennia is meaningless to God. All occurs in His ever-present moment. As the theologians say, "God lives in an eternal now."

In one sense, we share in God's time. All that is "real" to us is the now. Our past exists only in memories; our future doesn't yet exist. We experience life as a long string of present moments. I do remember a few things from my college minor in philosophy, if only enough to muddle my head.

So how does all this metaphysical lingo relate to you? Simply, what is long for you is not long for God. He hears your every prayer for your son, from your first to your someday last. Yet He obviously wants you to keep praying. He's said so repeatedly.

Jesus tells the parable of a "judge who neither feared God nor regarded man" (Luke 18:2). When a widow came seeking redress, the judge ignored her. Undeterred, she returned day after day until he finally answered her pleas (see Luke 18:1–5).

The lesson is not that God is some lofty judge who answers prayers only if He's nagged enough. The lesson is: Persevere in prayer. God understands better than we do how important something is. He wants us to understand it better too—not only in mind but in action. Persistent prayer must be very good for both the pray-er and the pray-ee, or else God wouldn't tell us to persist.

To use a popular phrase, "faith is a muscle." It is a commitment to act. By praying, you are being faithful. You are behaving as a mother who will do all she can for her child's spiritual well-being.

Feeling weary is understandable. It is an all too human reaction when a deep longing seems to be going unfulfilled. It is not, however, a sign of wearying faith.

Feelings are not the best guide to conduct. Your intent is to pray whether you feel like it or not. It is to seek God's guidance, whether you fathom it or not. It is a great act of faith to pray on when praying on seems to be changing nothing.

As you pray until the day you leave this earth, your son may still be distant from God. What will you see from Heaven? Changes you never saw on earth? Will your passing affect his soul, already softened by your many years of prayer? Much we can't foresee here.

Praying for another's conversion interacts with his free will. God does not force Himself on anyone. How He moves a soul remains a mystery. Still, He needs only the smallest opening to enter, one perhaps created by a mother's prayers.

# Dreaming of Sin

*Dear Dr. Ray,*

*I've been having a recurrent dream in which I'm committing a serious sin. It's not anything I have actually done or would do. Could this be a sign of some unconscious desire to commit this sin?*

*Night Mary*

In psychology school, I spent many waking hours thinking about dreams. What are they? Why do they happen? What do they mean?

In psychiatry's youth, dreams had much more status than they do today. Some argued that being asleep told more about one's psyche than did being awake. Freud called dreams the "royal road to the unconscious activities of the mind."[3] Because the psyche's defenses were half asleep, so to speak, one's forbidden desires and passions had a crack to poke through, although in twisted form. Hence the need for professional interpreters of dreams.

Though most clinicians no longer follow Freud, some of his ideas still reside in our culture's collective consciousness. The notion that dreams talk of one's inner life lingers.

---

[3]  Sigmund Freud, *The Interpretation of Dreams* (New York: Avon, 1965), 647.

What is a dream? The neurology behind dreams is still poorly understood. Research posits that dreams are a convoluted hodge-podge of preoccupations, recent thoughts, memories, and prior days' events. They are physiological stews that don't adhere to reality, as they flit erratically through associations, settings, and time. To recall a dream or its bits, one has to awaken during or shortly after it. When someone says, "I don't dream much," he's mistaken. Everybody dreams. What he's saying is that he sleeps soundly, with little arousal during the night. All that potential psychological grist left untapped!

Why do dreams happen? Freud and his colleagues maintained that dreams reveal the psyche. They light up one's inner life. That theory has pretty much fallen asleep. Dreams are now thought to serve some brain adaptation, though exactly what isn't clear. Perhaps they prune excess, unnecessary neural connections—redundancies. Or they simply reflect random brain activity, as the brain stays awake even while we're asleep. Whatever their origin, dreams don't unlock hidden realities as much as they muddle wide-awake ones.

What do my dreams mean? What do they say about me? Am I who I think I am, or could I be worse? This is the heart of your worry.

Your particular dream may not be unmasking a desire to sin but just the opposite: It reflects a strong desire *not* to sin. You actively reject this sin, but your mind has twisted that rejection out of shape. People dream about what disturbs them as well as what attracts them.

Perhaps this dream theme has been wired into your brain through mere repetition.

For years I've had a dream—nightmare—that is common to former college students. I'm back in school, it's late in the semester, and not only have I not once opened the textbook, but I haven't attended any classes. As I sit in the course for the very first time, I'm staring at an exam, totally clueless. Of course, my college courses did sometimes find me clueless, but I studied my way through them. How come that ending is never in my dream?

Why this dream now? At decades post-college, I'm not about to re-enroll, so I can't flunk out. I suspect the dream is an exaggeration of a once-upon-a-time worry that my brain has wired for replay. Upon waking up, I'm thankful I graduated. But now I am a little nervous that just writing about this dream will prompt a rerun tonight.

If your dream bothers you in the day, it's more likely to bother you at night. Don't fear the dream, and it will lose power. Shrug your shoulders about it. Take a tip from teens — "Whatever." Worrying about the dream may be the very emotion that spurs the dream.

Can dreams be occasions of sin? Morality 101 teaches that serious sin involves a conscious act. One must know something is wrong and then deliberately choose to do it anyway. Anything that interferes with free choice reduces personal blame.

A dream can be an indirect occasion of sin. An individual can desire the dream and take pleasure in having it. He can look forward to its next nocturnal visit. He can use it as fodder to daydream — that is, to relive the forbidden act in his mind without the real-life complications.

In essence, a dream can give someone permission to do something in fantasy that he wouldn't actually do. Given your dream distress, this wouldn't seem to be your case.

To repeat, you cannot sin while you're asleep. Dreams are random physiological phenomena rather than windows to the soul. What a dream says matters little. How we live when awake is what matters.

# Holier Pre-Kid

*Dear Dr. Ray,*

*Before I had children, I saw myself as a calm, easygoing person. Three kids later, I have a new self-image – a not so pretty one. I get upset more easily, scold more, and overall have to work harder to control my emotions. I think I could go to Confession every day.*

*Uneven Tempered*

Children are precious gifts of God, of infinite worth. They deserve all our love. Neither of which necessarily makes them easy to live with. How easy is it to live with someone who is immature, self-focused, rule-resistant, and guided by a juvenile conscience? The profile sounds unattractive, but it is the natural state of children, particularly younger ones.

At the core of the Christian worldview is fallen nature. All are born with a bent toward self, toward rebellion – toward sin. As G. K. Chesterton astutely observed, the doctrine of original sin is "the only part of Christian theology which can really be proved."[4]

---

[4] G. K. Chesterton, *Orthodoxy* (Radford, VA: Wilder Publications, 2008), 13.

Only with heavenly grace do we persevere in turning our self-will toward God's will. You talked about struggle in your question. And you're an adult, with decades of maturity, experience, self-examination, and motive to rein in your self. Were you to raise the most sweet, cooperative, loving children, you'd still do it with your very fallible humanness.

Fallen nature is at its most unruly at its youngest. Socializing and moralizing one's offspring takes the better part of two decades, with surprises, emotional jolts, and no shortage of annoyance along the way. How could frustration not intrude? How could you never raise your voice or say regrettable things? How could you not sin?

For most parents, the rewards far outweigh the hassles (especially looking back!). Still, there may be hassles that can be near occasions of sin. It is so much easier to be good when you don't share a roof with others—big or little. One saint, upon visiting her sister with a passel of children, is said to have been anxious to get back to the convent, where it was quieter, with less temptation to irritation.

It's not much of a challenge for me to love all the people in Australia. As far as I know, not one has ever done anything to personally make my life tougher. My sons and daughters? Now, that's an entirely different population. On most days, they resided twenty to fifty feet from me, while inhabiting the innermost precincts of my emotions. They set the conditions for me to sin more than all of Australia, India, and China combined, throwing in Bolivia and Iceland too.

Before being parents, most people underestimate the powerful emotions a child can evoke, positive and negative—irritation, disappointment, anger. So much do you want it to all go well that when it doesn't, well …

One definition of frustration: Frustration is the difference between the way we want things to be and the way they are. The bigger the gap, the more the frustration. To reduce frustration, it is generally easier to move expectations closer to reality than to move reality closer to expectations.

Kids are kids. (Am I profound, or what?) Reality says that kids act far from our expectations, in the near years anyway. Living within this reality lowers frustration, along with the temptation to act out that frustration.

Of course, you don't want to act your worst with your kids. Nonetheless, don't be discouraged by the "three steps forward, two steps back" trek to more calm, even-tempered motherhood. Sure, you will sin. But over time, you will likely sin less, especially as your kids move out.

Here's what worked for me: Post on the refrigerator a list of the Confession times at all the parishes within fifty miles. Or keep a priest on call twenty-four hours.

Part 6

# Family Friction

It's a given: Those closest to us have the most emotional effect on us, for better or worse. And for most people, those closest are family. It is disheartening when our deepest held beliefs are a source of friction between us and those we love.

Continuing to love in spite of religious differences and speaking the truth gently can close family divides and may even lead to a connection of minds and hearts.

# Don't Force It

*Dear Dr. Ray,*

*My daughter and her husband have two children, ages five and three. They are not raising the kids in the Church, as they were raised. When I try to pass on to my grandchildren some of the most basic faith practices – praying before meals, taking them to Mass when they are with me, giving them picture Bibles – my daughter gets upset and tells me I'm pushing my religion on her family.*

*Silenced Grandma*

Adult children who leave their childhood faith create ongoing disappointment, and often self-reproach, for their parents. What happened to my daughter on her way from my family to hers? How did she jettison what I taught her all those years? Will she ever embrace it again?

Any second-guessing is now intensified by watching your daughter raise her own children. Do you feel responsible for supposed failures in your parenting now being passed on to the next generation? Guilt over the past can push you to correct the present.

Your daughter's faith loss does not necessarily reflect how faithfully she was raised. Many factors influence someone's move away from God. (See "Two out of Three?" in part 8.)

However well-intentioned you are, you face an obstacle: Your daughter doesn't agree. Her resistance may be not only about your religion but about her parenting—that is, about its perceived deficiencies. She hears your saying meal blessings as your way to fill in her family's religious gaps.

You are Grandma, but she is Mom. However misguided you believe she is, she has the right to parent her way. By going against her, not only could you antagonize her, but you could push her and her husband further from the Faith. Your daughter could also limit your time with the kids if she sees no other way to restrain you. Softening your daughter's attitude is difficult, if not impossible, if she feels you are ignoring or defying her.

Therefore, cease your religious guidance. Apologize to your daughter and husband for not respecting their wishes. Assure them also that you will never do anything with which they would disagree. To make any religious inroads, you must first have a solid relationship. It's the base from which you may one day be able to teach freely.

What about your Christian call to share the Faith? You can't impose something that isn't wanted. What if the kids want it? Even so, their mother doesn't, and she is deciding for them, right now anyway.

Still, you can teach your grandchildren the Faith. How? Be loving and easy to get along with. The children—and their mother—will see Grandma as a really neat lady, who is religious. The combination is winsome.

Through it all, don't lose hope. Many adult children return to the Church upon realizing the worth of giving their own children something more than this world's philosophy. The kids lead them home.

# Forbidden Fruit

*Dear Dr. Ray,*

*Our sixteen-year-old daughter is smitten with an eighteen-year-old boy whom my husband and I know to be a troubled young man. I want to curtail their contact, but my husband says to let things run their course or we'll just make the relationship a forbidden fruit.*

*Swallowing Hard*

Biblical in its imagery, "forbidden fruit" has come to mean "something that looks pleasing because it is denied." Even if that something is not healthy for us, we want it because we can't have it.

Our first parents had the pick of nearly anything in Paradise. The whole garden was theirs to enjoy, with one exception. The tree that God commanded them to leave alone, they didn't. They tasted its fruit, with world-altering repercussions.

We, their descendants, are wounded morally by their disobedience and are thus attracted to much we should leave alone. When we see this inclination in our descendants — our children — we worry: By forbidding something they desire, will we make it all the more desirable?

Out-of-reach fruit may look the sweetest, especially to young eyes. Someone with more mature eyes (read "parent") must sometimes keep it out of reach. The child's well-being demands it.

Parents have to make years of judgments, guided by what is good, not by how much a child wants it or could react if denied it. A five-year-old craves sugar-loaded cereal for breakfast. By denying him, will you start him on the path to a calorie-crazed adulthood stuffed with jumbo, jelly-filled donuts? A fourteen-year-old daughter is nagging to spend time with the older neighbor boy, at his house, alone. Will a "No way" only provoke sneakiness? A college sophomore living at home for the summer sees no problem whatsoever in sampling vile video games. Will your "Absolutely not" drive him deeper into virtual unreality, if not at your house, then someday at his?

Much that looks delicious to children will make them sick. A parent must decide what fruit to allow when, and how much. Rare is the child who needs little protection from his appetites. And where these appetites threaten morals and character, a parent has to be steadfast.

Dad wants to let the relationship run its course. To where? And who's driving? Can you know how it all will end? Who could get hurt on its way forward or backward? As my grandmother would say, "Better you cry now than we both cry later."

Your husband may have faith that your daughter will eventually see this young man as you do. Maybe so, but again, at what cost? What complications could arise in the meantime?

Farsighted parenting involves having a plan B. Your husband will likely agree with it; your daughter, likely not—though she may be forced to accept it if she sees it as her only option. Allow limited, closely supervised boy-girl contact, with you and Dad as the supervisors. This may happen only at your home or perhaps on a double date, with you and Dad as the doubles. Uh huh.

Plan B has two upsides. One, in a morally safe setting, your daughter will better assess the character of this relationship. Two, this young man may seek other gardens, having decided you are a bit too forbidding for his tastes.

My belly tells me the latter will happen before the former.

# Too Many Channels

*Dear Dr. Ray,*

*My father lets my sons, ages ten and twelve, watch television shows at his house that I would never approve of. He argues, "It's not going to hurt them."*

*A Different View*

"It's not going to hurt them" has variants: "It's not like they're going to be criminals." "That's real life — they'll see lots of it." "You can't shelter them forever." "They're good kids — they can handle it."

To this last one, one mother answered, "I think they're good kids too, and I'd like to keep them that way."

In teaching virtue, the question is not "What harm will it do?" It is "What good will it do?" Humans can survive all manner of threats and assaults. That doesn't mean they are good for us. Most of the time, the body neutralizes life-endangering germs. Are these germs then of no concern?

When I was fourteen, I fell face-first down a flight of stairs while carrying two folding chairs under each arm. (Macho teen boy, anyone?) I didn't touch anything until I hit the concrete floor.

Except for a bruised ego, I walked away unscathed. Did this prove that similar future shortcuts would be harmless?

"It won't hurt them" is one rationale for indifference. It says, "It takes too much effort to supervise this." If I can convince myself that kids are naturally resilient to technological toxins, I won't have to be quite so vigilant. And I won't have to weather their upset over my vigilance.

Your dilemma is not caused by your father's attitude. He can have his opinion; you don't have to abide by it. He may believe he must give the boys some cultural normalcy because their parents don't. He must compensate for your overprotectiveness. If you're going to be out of step with the crowd, he won't be.

Your dilemma is caused by your father's behavior. Whether intending to or not, he is sending your sons the message, "Your parents are wrong; I'll correct it when you're with me." Not only is he undercutting you at his place, but he's making life tougher for you at yours. Your sons could resent that you aren't as TV-cool as Grandpa. After all, he's a grown-up too, and one who has been around a lot longer than you. He should know more about this TV thing.

Have you talked with your dad about why you raise the boys as you do—not just your television stance but overall? How definite have you been? Does he understand that TV monitoring is one of your nonnegotiables?

He doesn't have to agree, just cooperate. How can you confirm that? Without being in Grandpa's house, you can't. He and the boys could form a sort of viewers' conspiracy. One ally for you, however, is time.

Kids aren't the best at keeping secrets secret. TV viewing will be broadcast in their actions: acting out the pictures they've seen, using vocabulary foreign to your home but native to TV.

Should Grandpa insist on offering unlimited channels, he has limited your actions. You'll have to figure out how to supervise not only your sons but your father. Perhaps this means visiting Grandpa only as a family, or one parent always accompanying the boys. It's sad when a parent has to take such action, but your father is forcing it—that is, unless you are willing to lower your standards.

"Honor thy father and mother" means giving parents the respect and love that are their due. It does not mean that you have to abide by their every request and decision. Nor does raising your children have to be in line with their ideas.

Others don't always agree with vigilant parenting. And sometimes those others are one's own parents.

Whatever happened to the days when grandparents only sneaked the kids a second helping of ice cream—after they finished their fourth cookie?

# Whom Do You Trust?

*Dear Dr. Ray,*

*We supervise our daughter far more than her friends' parents do their children. She says, "You just don't trust me." We need an answer.*

*The Hawks*

How short an answer do you need? How about "I trust you; I don't trust the world." If you want something longer, I suspect your daughter won't accept it any better than my pithy sound bite.

You could say, "Oh, but I do trust you. I trust that you are fifteen. And I trust that fifteen-year-olds think like fifteen-year-olds. And I trust that there will be situations that, for all your wisdom, you can't handle. And I trust that with time, I'll allow you to experience more. And I trust that you'll believe me when I tell you I'm doing this out of love and to protect you."

How could she not be moved by such a heartfelt expression of trust?

If, after all this, your daughter still wants to equate your supervision with no trust, so be it. It's not that you don't respect her maturity. It's that you understand her youth. She's trying to make you feel guilty by turning a positive (sound parental judgment) into a negative (a personal insult).

Why are kids so quick to take our loving conduct personally? For one, humans of all ages are quick to take another's behavior personally. Call it the sensitivity of the self.

For another, teens especially are quick to misunderstand parents' motives. What you are doing comes from your underestimating them. You just don't realize yet how trustworthy and downright grown-up they are. The problem, dear parent, lies in your misperception, not in their youth.

"You just don't trust me" may be true; you don't fully trust them. And so? Incomplete trust isn't a bad thing, socially or psychologically. A smart parent realizes the limits of a child's judgment, experience, and character. Even the most mature fifteen-year-old is still a fifteen-year-old.

Other parents might be fueling your daughter's fire. They're letting their kids do too much too soon. As your daughter sees it, if all those grown-ups are more "trusting" than you, you are the suspicious one. How could all of them be wrong and you alone be right? If this were a game, the score would be twenty-three (other parents) to two (you and your spouse).

Even if the score were 123 parents to you, you'd still win. Good parenting isn't done by group vote. The question is not "How do my standards line up with others?" The question is "How do my standards help me raise my child best?"

Believing that your daughter's friends have too much freedom too early, you'll parent unlike others. Your daughter won't always understand. Someday she will, and that's what matters.

For now, the only foolproof way to convince your daughter that you do trust her is to give her all the trust she wishes. But that's not a trustworthy way to parent.

# To Love, Not Condone

*Dear Dr. Ray,*

*At age twenty-one, my daughter moved in with her boyfriend. My husband and I didn't raise her to do that. It's been over a year, and I'm still uneasy around them.*

*Troubled*

How uneasy are you, and how much does your daughter—her boyfriend too—sense it? Are your times together tense and, consequently, less? The course of an uneasy relationship is toward dwindling contact.

You wish to stay close to your daughter, even as she continues to stay so close to her boyfriend. And you wish not to condone their housekeeping. How do you balance both?

The broader question: How does one love another without accepting wrong conduct? It's a question forced upon Christians repeatedly.

Above all, we are called to love, to treat others—the moral and the not so—with dignity and decency. We are also called to live by clear-cut standards, not ours but God's. And these standards don't solely benefit believers but all people.

At any time, for any reason, anyone can choose to neglect or reject God's standards and expect us to accept, even celebrate, their choices. The great irony is that someone can ask, yes, demand, that another be tolerant of her moral position but will be most intolerant of their moral position about her moral position.

Your daughter knows what you believe. No doubt, you've told her in one way or another throughout the past year. And you raised her that way for twenty years prior to that. It's not that she doesn't understand. It's that she's chosen to live counter to those beliefs, for now anyway.

The time to broach the matter is over. Should your daughter do so, then the door is open. Reopen it yourself, and you'll probably just open up more emotional distance between you. Conversations get stiff when one or more parties anticipate a touchy subject lurking just around the next sentence.

Could your daughter hear your reticence as acceptance? Shouldn't you say something every few visits or so, just to remind her that you're not growing indifferent to her playing house? Couldn't she get the impression that her arrangement is all right by you?

Not likely. You have too much shared history for that.

Suppose, however, she does conclude that your moral vision is blurring. It's in her interest to think so. At that, you are under no moral obligation to repeatedly reiterate your stance. You are responsible to communicate it, and you have done so over many years. You are not responsible for your daughter's misreading why you're saying no more.

The religious leaders of Our Lord's day censured Him because He ate with tax collectors, who were considered among the most despicable of sinners. Dining at the same table wasn't seen as a friendly get-together; it bespoke deep fellowship. Scripture doesn't report Jesus admonishing, "Okay, guys, don't think any of this means I approve of what you're doing. And you've got two weeks to forsake it, or you won't be seeing me around here anymore." No, the sinners and everybody else knew where Jesus stood; nonetheless, He continued to reach out to them.

Your love for your daughter—and her boyfriend—is your best means to morally move them. Without a decent relationship, you won't have much of a chance to persuade. Whether one day she and her boyfriend break up, marry, or separate domiciles, you want your mother-daughter bridge to her to remain intact, with no lingering resentments toward you. You'll also be protecting yourself from any attitude of "Oh, now you're going to be warm toward me because I'm good again."

As you pray for your daughter's change of heart, pray too that your heart never changes toward her.

# The College Experience

*Dear Dr. Ray,*

*Our daughter graduates from high school this year. She is adamant about living on a college campus, and the farther away, the better. She wants the "college experience." My wife and I have strong reservations about this. We'd prefer she attend college nearby and live at home.*

*Experienced Dad*

Some forty-plus years ago, I had the college experience, nearly a decade's worth. Did I rush into freedom? Face-first. Did I come, go, sleep, wake on my own cycle? Sure did. Did I chase fun? Yep. Did my religion become more self-defined? Afraid so.

In the 1970s, my college persona was the norm. Today it wouldn't be. It would be a little too restrained.

Not many would dispute that the college social scene has decayed dramatically since my generation. Alcohol, drugs, sex, parties, rock and roll—all are attending school daily alongside the students. Some kids pilot the shoals and graduate afloat. Many—surveys say half or more—pass their courses but flunk the morals and faith taught for years by their families.

Once upon a time, institutes of higher learning wore the mantle of *in loco parentis* ("in place of the parent" for those of you who overslept Latin class). They took seriously their role in guiding and supervising young adults. Many schools now seem to practice *in absentia parentis*. They ally with the students, not with the parents. They let young people discover—some would say "stumble"—their way forward. The results of this philosophical shift have not been pretty.

All this is not to paint a bleak and scary picture. It's to paint a real one for parents as a teen nears college.

If you lived on campus back when, don't use your experience to predict your daughter's. Because you landed upright (does your wife want to gather the relatives and vote on that?), you can't assume your daughter will too.

"But she really wants to go." No doubt. But as my little sister used to retort when we argued, "So?" Children really want all kinds of things—some good, some really bad. A parent has to help them decide which is which and sometimes has to make the decision for them. You can't foresee your daughter's future, so you're forced to make a judgment call. Do kids like parents' judgment calls? Only those in their favor.

You have "strong reservations." Is one of them related to your daughter's level of maturity and trustworthiness? The best predictor of future behavior is past behavior in similar situations. Your daughter hasn't yet lived on a campus; she has lived in a far more supervised setting—home. How has she done?

Some kids can be trusted solo on a Bahamian cruise. Others, not in the next room. How your daughter has behaved the last few years is one good gauge of how she'll behave in the next few.

In addition to moral and social questions, there is an economic one: Who is the bank? You? Even partially? This gives you a veto vote in her college choice. But perhaps your daughter will pay for everything—tuition, room and board, books, insurance, car, cell phone, curling iron, whatever. As a legal-aged adult, she can thus attend where she chooses.

My oldest daughter, Hannah, was attracted to a leadership training curriculum at an all-female college out of state. Knowing our position—you live here, we pay; you live there, you pay (no loans)—she enrolled in ROTC at the college, graduating as an officer in the army, her desired career. Three of our other children attended colleges within commuting distance. All four graduated with a priceless life lesson: "No loans is good."

Speaking of money, statistics indicate that up to half of college graduates don't end up working in their chosen major. Many find jobs that don't require a degree and barely cover living expenses, much less loan payments stretching into social security. For several years, they enjoyed faux-independence, only to move back to dependence—Mom and Dad's place. Their youth made them financially shortsighted. You are older and more clear-eyed about money matters.

A college-near-home stance has exceptions. Certain technical or specialized degrees might be available only beyond commuting distance. Generous scholarship awards from colleges are a plus. Catholic and other private traditional schools may offer a faith-building and moral education, a college experience that would teach with you rather than against you.

Your instincts are pushing you hard in one direction. Your daughter is pushing you hard in another. When a parent ignores or suppresses his strong instincts, one reason is fear of a child's reaction. Will she be resentful? Will she rebel? Will she move out? (Is that a problem?)

Any of these could happen—likely temporarily—but none justify allowing something that you believe is risky.

Part 7

# The New Moral Normal

It's a tug-of-war. At one end are those who assert, "This is the way the world now is. Children have to learn how to live in it." At the other end are those who counter, "Children need more time to morally mature before having to learn how to live in it."

So who sets the pace for learning? Society, with its ever-lowering standards? Or a parent, who, in slowing the pace and protecting innocence, may feel out of rhythm with society?

Conventional thinking says: Kids have to navigate the world as it now is. Conventional thinking isn't always wisdom.

# Protective Parents

*Dear Dr. Ray,*

*My four children are all under age eleven. Others have called me a protective parent, and it's not typically meant as a compliment. I just don't want my kids growing up too fast.*

*Mama Lion*

By "protective," you're not saying that you shield your children from all the natural, age-related fallout of their conduct? You're not driving an emotional bulldozer in front of them, sweeping away every rock and bump. Instead, you mean that you want to give them a few more years of childhood and a few less years of premature adulthood.

Modern child-raising theories have turned much long-believed wisdom on its head. Not so long ago, parents were indeed to "overprotect" their children, not only from lions and tigers and bears but from seeing too much worldly ugliness too early. Childhood innocence was a treasure to be guarded and nurtured.

Only recently have those who resist society's rush to "socialize" at younger ages been questioned, scorned even, as though stunting their children's psychological growth. "You can't protect them forever." "That's a tough world out there." "They've got to learn to deal with life."

No, you can't protect them forever. Yes, the world is tough. And yes, children do have to deal with it. But wise parents don't want to shelter their children always and everywhere, keeping them holed up socially until Independence Day. They want to shelter them—emotionally and morally—longer than the new cultural norm says to.

Anytime you hear the word "protection" used, ask: Protection from what, when, and for how long? The final answers are all yours. Others—including many so-called experts—will push you to move with the crowd's pace. A wise parent sets the pace based upon her family's values and her child's maturity.

Much that is supposedly normal—according to society, that is—is not necessarily good. The majority of teens have televisions in their bedrooms. Nearly all twelve-year-olds have smartphones. Most kids drive the day their age allows. Are these norms to reflexively follow because the numbers command it? How did consensus become the path to virtue?

"Protective" is a relative term. The most sheltered ten-year-old of today has seen and heard more social pollution than the typical fourteen-year-old of three generations ago. Back then, you wouldn't have been called "protective"; you would have been called responsible. Are you overprotective, or do you just look so when compared to those who are underprotective?

The notion is widespread: Children are faced with more adult realities these days, so they'd best face them sooner rather than later. Supposedly, somehow a child is better able to adjust if he adjusts younger. He'll have more years to learn to cope. Some child-rearing notions I can only respond to with "Huh?"

Who is more able to navigate social trickiness—a well-raised ten-year-old or a well-raised fourteen-year-old? The older the child, the more his internal resources handle what comes at him. Postponing the day of moral testing does not arrest a child's development; it gives him time to ready himself for the test.

Next time you're accused of being a protective parent—code for "overprotective parent"—answer, "You're right. I want to be. I want to give my kids a childhood while they're still children."

# Teach Me about This, Mom

*Dear Dr. Ray,*

*My brother tells me I should let my children watch morally borderline TV shows so I can use them as "teachable moments." Have you heard this phrase?*

*Uneducated*

"Teachable *moment*" is a trendy term. It refers to using a situation, experience, or problem to teach a child something worthwhile. It means drawing a good lesson from some circumstances, good or bad.

Good parents teach to the moment all the time. They take advantage of natural openings to instruct or correct. Mom and little Rocky are watching a cartoon about a car-eating space invader. (Whatever happened to simple good and bad guys, like Popeye and Bluto?) Assuming she can wrest Rocky's attention from the TV for six seconds, Mom slips in a question or two about seeing the story with a good moral eye. Here the teachable moment helps form character.

Your brother is stretching the concept. He says to expose your children to something questionable so you can ask questions about it. Really, he's saying, "Let's talk about how what you're watching is not good for you."

Most information enters through our eyes. At any instant, we see much more than we hear. Words matter, but as the most novice ad person knows, the vision can outtalk the best of slogans.

"A picture is worth a thousand words." Formerly, this adage referred to basic, two-dimensional reproductions. Our ancestors revered the power of images, even back when they were very imperfect reflections of reality. Today, with computer-created anything, a picture is worth a million words. Our techno world has fashioned images that seem more real than reality itself.

Pornography is a tragic example. A devastating effect of viewing pornography is that the pictures are seared into the mind's eye, becoming tenacious residents of one's storehouse of memories. It is far better never to have seen these images than to try to delete them with after-the-moment discussions. Even with the best professional counseling, this can be an uphill slog.

The serious flaw in the teaching-moment concept: The more intensely negative an image or experience, the less we can draw something positive from it.

Some people advocate a more moderate stance: Create teachable moments but not recklessly. Don't throw children into the deep end of life's pool. Let them wade into shallow water holding your hand.

Cautions are still warranted. For one, a parent might not want her child to get wet yet. She knows the pool will still be open when her child is a better swimmer. No need to venture into deeper water just to teach that it's deep.

For another, how a given moment will affect a given child is hard to anticipate. Even twins can react quite differently to the same experience. Storm weathers it with little afterthought, while

Sunny bakes in it for the next three hours, cries himself to sleep, and has dark dreams for a week straight. The only way to know for sure how teachable a moment will be is to let it happen. And that might prove costly.

Here is my teaching for the moment. Don't let your children be exposed to anything you think will be premature, given their ages and innocence. Every parent has limitless teaching opportunities without adding any that will force her to teach something before its time.

# Rebellion Risk?

*Dear Dr. Ray,*

*We're a young family trying to raise our children with strong standards. We've been told that if our standards are too high, our kids will rebel.*

*Highly Skeptical*

Your standards are too high? How do you measure that? Can you poll a hundred people for a consensus? And what if you desire to live higher than most?

The only way, it seems, to judge if you're pushing your family's moral bar out of reach is to watch whether your kids try to jump over it or limbo under it. Then you'll know. Not really.

"High standards" is not an absolute phrase. It is a relative one. A standard can look extreme when compared with a group standard that has slipped. Many now measure moral correctness by what is defined as the norm. That is, normal is right. If the norm is unhealthy, however, then what is healthy can look abnormal.

The notion that high standards risk rebellion has gotten lots of momentum from the professionals. (Just because someone gets paid for giving advice doesn't mean the advice is always good.) Recently, I attended a meeting in which one therapist, whose specialty was adolescents, proclaimed authoritatively, "We all know that all teens will rebel if a parent's standards are too high." Were I feeling more rebellious, I would have countered, "No, we don't all know that, and all teens won't rebel." Call it my inner adolescent.

The therapist's warning is one of those sophisticated new insights that have overturned long-standing common sense. Not all that long ago, the principle was "the higher the standards, the better." Lowered standards led to poorer living. Of late, we've bought into the reverse: High standards can lead to poor living.

This fallacy finds face in the stereotype of the preacher's kid. Everyone knows that he's the most morally unprincipled kid in the whole congregation. Saying yes to his dad's teaching, he says no to living it and flies low under the parental radar.

What "everyone knows," though, turns out to be more often false than true. The exception has birthed the rule. In fact, most preachers' kids grow up to reflect, not reject, their upbringing.

Jesus said, "You ... must be perfect, as your heavenly Father is perfect" (Matt. 5:48). Perfect? Such a nonnegotiable word. Is Jesus teaching that the only path to Heaven lies in keeping impossibly high precepts? Or is He encouraging us to stretch toward those precepts?

More than anyone, Jesus understood the frailty of fallen human nature. He also knew that, because of our frailty, we need clear ideals.

How does a parent lower a moral bar that she worries is too high? "You should always tell the truth, Truman, but 'always' does seem a bit demanding, so how about a maximum of two lies a week, three if they're small." "Always treat your sister with respect, Justice, but if you feel you can't, at least try not to curse at her." "We realize, Chastity, that our 'no dating until seventeen' rule is stricter than most other parents'. So you can start texting relationships at age fourteen."

To compromise a standard, one has to allow exceptions to it. And the exceptions weaken its spirit.

As said, many young adults are forsaking, at least in part, their parents' moral teachings. This is often thought to signal that the kids couldn't meet family expectations; therefore, they renounced them. An understandable reaction but an often wrong interpretation. Grown children leave the Faith for myriad reasons—cultural forces preeminent. Shedding the yoke of binding standards is not high on their list.

Kids rebel against standards that they neither fully understand nor appreciate. Young minds routinely judge the most reasonable principles as too demanding or unjust. That's because most kids survey what their peers are allowed to do and think, "How can all those parents be wrong and my parents be right?" Only when they look back with adult vision, especially that magnified by raising their own children, do they come to realize how right their parents were.

Then too, the best guidance is loving guidance. As Josh McDowell, a Christian author and speaker, says, "Rules without relationship breed rebellion."[5] A rigid code of conduct enforced with little love and affection is asking for resistance. It is a "my way or the highway" style rather than benevolent teaching.

High standards are most durably imparted when wrapped in spoken and unspoken "I love yous." A child who feels valued is far more open to being taught values.

Too, your children are not walking the high moral plane all alone. You're walking with them. Your standards are not only for little people but for big people as well. Elevated standards raise everybody.

---

[5] Josh McDowell, "Rules without Relationships Lead to Rebellion," Josh McDowell Ministry, YouTube video, 2:27, https://www.you tube.com/watch?v=Tx1SOiawASw.

# Beyond the Three R's

*Dear Dr. Ray,*

*My fifth-grade daughter's health class has an upcoming one-week section on sexual education. I've looked at the material, and it is very explicit, especially for a ten-year-old. It also presents a moral perspective far different from our own. Options?*

*Prudish Parent*

Once upon a time, on a planet far away, schools concentrated on shaping young minds through the three R's—reading, 'riting, and 'rithmetic. Education in attitudes, morals, and character were subjects for the parents' classroom. Schools assisted, but only within a family's framework.

Nowadays, a new letter has been added to the scholastic alphabet. We now have the three S's—Safe sex, Save the earth, and Say no to drugs. And these letters don't always spell good words for parents, particularly parents who are religious.

Two plus two equals four. The speed of light is 186,000 miles per second. Babe Ruth was the greatest baseball player of all time. These are indisputable truths. (All right, maybe it's Mickey Mantle.) One can disagree with them only if he wishes to dispute reality.

On the other hand, teaching when, how, and with whom to have sexual relations; presenting the perils of cocaine; discerning whether a five-child family is hogging a disproportionate share of the earth's oxygen—these are matters of moral judgment, sometimes scientific debate. And the best age for their introduction varies widely from child to child.

The argument is, though such questions are best answered at home, too many homes ignore them. For good or ill, the assignment then falls to the schools, next in line for socializing. Sadly, there is truth to this. Some parents are more than content to let the schools teach not only the three R's but the three S's as well. Even so, plenty of mothers and fathers still want to instill their own family's values and not those of a textbook, especially a textbook with a decidedly anti-religious worldview.

Another argument: Schools need to form the whole child—that is, teach him not just how to read and write but how to think rightly. If thinking rightly means training in logic and reason, I couldn't agree more. But if it means instructing a new and better way to live, I couldn't agree less. Who decides what is new and better? Who decides what it means to think rightly morally? An author? An expert? An atheist? Or a parent, with the God-given responsibility to teach what is right—that is, what she believes is the best way for her child to live?

On to your dilemma. First step: Pull together the textbook's most controversial or offensive passages, as you see them—on one page if possible. Show them to any other parents you think would be interested in reading up close what their ten- or eleven-year-olds are expected to read and believe. Likely, many, if not most, will be unaware of the material.

Next, meet with the teacher, the principal, or both. Most educators are open to a parent's concerns. However, most are not open to altering subject matter because of one voice. If other parents are with you, your voice will echo.

Don't verbally pounce. Don't dispute—not at the moment you walk in the door, anyway. As reasonable as your points might be, you'll risk sounding unreasonable and lacking in credibility.

You are there first to ask questions, to hear the school's rationale. Why is this subject matter presented at this grade level? What if the values conveyed are different from a parent's? Are there ways to keep a student innocent about these topics a while longer?

The administrator might understand, even agree, with your perspective but not have the authority to change the curriculum. Likewise, the teacher could be sympathetic; perhaps he or she also thinks the material is questionable and, after hearing from you or others, might find ways to teach it at a level more age-suitable. Having the principal and teacher philosophically allied with you almost always makes for a workable solution.

Whether the school agrees with you or not, it will probably accept a compromise. For example, your daughter might be permitted to quietly slip out of class to another place: the library, the cafeteria, an office, or a study hall. If the principal or teacher doesn't suggest this, you can. As the parent, you have the final authority.

Your daughter may be thrilled about skipping health class, but she may not be thrilled about looking like a social oddball. No matter how quiet her exit, other kids may notice her absence every day, same time and same subject. Any snide remarks about little Miss Purity and Mrs. Purity, her saintly mother, could talk her into staying glued to her seat. And she might not read from the same parenting page as you.

A good explanation: "Some things are not appropriate for you to study at your age. And some of what the school book offers goes against what we believe as a family. As your mom and dad, we have to judge what is good for you to know and when.

"Next week, your health class will cover some subjects we don't believe are right for you at age ten. So we've set it up with your teacher that you will leave class during that time and go to another place in the school. Questions?"

Clear. Rational. Sensitive. You should hear, "Oh, Mother, I was hoping you'd say this. I do so wish to stay a child longer, and I recognize that your way is the best way, even if all my friends and their parents think otherwise."

Okay, back to earth. Should your daughter be upset with the arrangement, repeat your mini speech every morning and evening until she agrees. Just joshing. Don't overexplain. Don't debate. Just make it happen. You are looking out for your daughter's long-term health.

The good news? Your daughter will probably stay upset for only the next week or so. Then she'll start asking what other classes she can skip.

# May I Skip This Dance?

*Dear Dr. Ray,*

*My son's school is holding its annual dance for eighth-graders. His mother and I think he's too young to go. We're surprised at the pressure on us to relent, not only from our son but from friends and others at the school.*

*Dancing Solo*

Some years ago, a survey of middle- and high-school students revealed that a child whose first date (remember "dating"?) came between ages eleven and thirteen had a 90 percent chance of being sexually active by senior year. A first date at age fourteen: 50 percent chance. First date at sixteen: 20 percent. There's a straight-line correlation: The earlier a child is introduced to one-on-one relationships, the sooner he moves to full physical relations.

When I present these numbers to parent groups, the gasps are audible. The predominant thought: "Who would let a child date so young?" To which I answer, "Many, if not most, middle schools and junior highs sponsor dances."

One could argue that these dances aren't really dates but supervised get-togethers. Even so, they are introductions to the dating scene. And why wouldn't some kids push to make the dance a date? After all, the school set it up. What's the problem?

Admittedly, the chances of a boy-girl stealthy tryst in this setting may be low, assuming the adult supervision is high. Some would argue that these dances are safe, early exposure to the opposite sex. In other words, "What's the harm?"

In forming morals, the foremost query is not "What's the harm?" but "What's the good?" Is low risk a good reason to encourage something that (for other reasons) is happening too soon?

Once upon a time, group socials were a natural step toward courting. The contact was communal, the dance partners were older than twelve, and the grown-ups made sure that contacts were kept innocent. These days, anyone overseeing a supposedly innocent junior-high dance is forced to admit that the apparel alone is anything but innocent.

"It's not anything they don't see elsewhere." Sadly true. None-theless, shouldn't adults protect childhood innocence where they can, rather than moving in concert with the culture's hypersexual-izing pace?

To claim that young people are growing up sexually no faster today than yesterday is to ignore the statistics. Casual sex, out-of-wedlock pregnancies, sexual diseases—all have exploded in the past few decades. The forces driving this cultural decay are manifold, but a potent one is the age plummet of opposite-sex titillation.

The question is not "Does your son notice girls?" Of course he does. The question is "At what speed do you want your son to act on his awareness?" At society's? Or at yours?

Because you want a slower pace than the new norm, you'll get pressure from all sides. Your son will push on you; you can expect that. What he sees—besides all the cute girls—is a whole crowd of grown-ups who don't think as you do. And these adults, parents too, will pressure you. The key to standing strong is knowing: You are the parent; these decisions are yours, not the group's. You know your son best. You know the morals you wish to teach and when. Moving with the crowd will lower their pressure on you. Less pressure, however, is no sign you're acting wisely. Parenting by moral consensus is not a good way to parent. The consensus that matters is yours and your spouse's.

Likely, you have more allies at your son's school than it appears. Other parents would like to get their kids off society's sexual fast-forward but are too intimidated to resist. They admire you, perhaps at a distance, perhaps silently. Your confidence will stiffen their spines.

# Cell-Phone Romance

*Dear Dr. Ray,*

*We just discovered that, for the last two months, our thirteen-year-old daughter has been texting a boy from another school. He's become the center of her emotional world.*

*Read Enough*

Mother, may I take a giant step backward? (Remember "Mother May I?"—back when kids played games face-to-face?) Why does your daughter have a cell phone, and how long has she had one? A cell phone in the hands of a socially impulsive youngster (read "adolescent") calls for trouble.

Parents worry most about major misuses: sexting, prurient pictures, Internet carousing, minute-by-minute texting. These happen often enough, but as you've experienced firsthand, the potential for relational complications rises with hands-on time on the phone.

Smartphones can connect kids pretty much to anyone, anytime, anywhere. And the connection is one that the most vigilant parent can't completely monitor. Only when a bad connection becomes clear is the parent called to answer the phone trouble.

This is not to say, "I told you so." Actually, I never told you so. But it is a first step toward solving your dilemma—one that calls for a wholesale rethinking of your phone terms.

No doubt your daughter sees her phone as her love line to her boyfriend as well as her indispensable peer link. "How can I talk to my friends without my phone? That's how everybody talks now! I might as well forget about having any friends."

Wow! Social isolation is just a dead battery away. Do you forbid your daughter to speak to her friends face-to-face? Are there real live humans at her school? Do you still have—gasp!—a landline? Carrier pigeons? Is any one of these person-to-person interactions off-limits to your daughter? Okay, the pigeons do need some training.

So why does the smartphone drown out her every other mode of communication? Because it's peer approved, 24-7 accessible, and private—all at the top of a thirteen-year-old's social list.

Bad news and good news. The bad news: Your daughter believes she now has an emotional attachment to this young boy. I mean, how could she not after ten-thousand-plus text messages? For most kids, a mere five thousand adds up to a techno-marriage.

The good news: Pulling the phone's plug—er, charger—could allow this romance to drop from loss of signal, especially since the kids do not have everyday contact at school. Of course, this is assuming your daughter doesn't have unlimited access to e-mail, an iPad, a Twitter account, and Facebook. These, too, need close watching and perhaps a shutdown. Kids are pros at navigating the wireless world, going where they want and with whom, all under their parents' radar.

Your daughter could commandeer the phone of any friend who agrees that you and your spouse are total Pony Express throwbacks. That would include pretty much anyone her age. Still, without personal ownership of a phone, her contact time should decline.

That, or her phone boyfriend may pursue other contacts: eighth-grade girls with no phone limits whatsoever.

Are you blocking the problem but not resolving it? I don't know. (How much did you pay for this book?) The answer depends upon your daughter's feelings, her resentment at being denied them, her ingenuity at circumventing your blockade, and the boy's perseverance. Even so, most premature romances feed on an uninterrupted connection. Without it, one or both parties hang it up.

Many so-called experts would caution against pulling the phone. (Probably most don't have teenagers.) They would intone about the fruit forbidden, the futility of straining to cool youthful feelings, the temptation to sneakiness, and damage to the parent-child relationship. Yes, these could be complications, but what is your alternative?

Persuasion? "Honey, don't you think you're a little too young to be this involved with someone? Do you really know this boy? Do his parents know about you two?" Adolescents would have a range of comebacks to these queries, but most could be summarized with "No, yes, and yes."

Do parents allow risky behavior to continue for fear of a child's reaction to their stopping it? Once a youngster has set a course, must a parent watch it unfold, hoping it will pass without too many untoward consequences? Sometimes kids force parents to take a stand that causes static in the short-term but silences it in the long run.

Your daughter's text-bonding signals a broader question: Why a cell phone at her age?

# Socialized? By Whom?

*Dear Dr. Ray,*

*I'm a homeschooling mom of four. If I'm asked one more time, "What about their socialization?" I think I'm going to say something really unsociable.*

*Silent So Far*

You're on the receiving end of the number-one cliché thrown at homeschooling parents. The question sounds questioning, but it can be debunked from many directions.

Homeschooled kids are neither raised nor educated on Saturn. Most have brothers and sisters; many have several. Most live in neighborhoods of people, who talk to them even. They are active with other homeschoolers through field trips, courses, and co-ops. Their world is not a social vacuum.

At a large homeschooling conference, Bill Bennett, the former Secretary of Education, was asked to answer to what homeschoolers call the "S question." He succinctly replied, "Socialization to what?" Meaning, "socialization" has little meaning without defining what kind of socialization.

When I'm asked the "S question," I ask back, "What do you mean?" (Isn't that just like a shrink?) Do you mean the teaching of good conduct, morals, and character? That is, and always has been, the foremost responsibility of parents. Or do you mean learning the social rules of twenty same-aged peers? Maneuvering through the peer world is a skill, to be sure. It is, however, only a sliver of what could be labeled "socialization."

Many parents homeschool because they want to be the ones to socialize their children. They want to raise their kids at their moral pace, not the culture's. They don't consider the young crowd a trustworthy guide to good living. So when asked, "What about their socialization?" they can reply, "That's exactly why I'm homeschooling."

"Children need to learn how to get along with all kinds of people. They need to experience the push and pull of social negotiating."

True, but how are they best equipped to do that? From children, who may be either pro-socializing or de-socializing? Or from adults, who just might know more about qualities such as tolerance, kindness, and responsibility?

For almost all of human history, across almost all cultures, there was no universal childhood education. In this country, the effort is barely three lifetimes old. How, then, were children socialized prior to the advent of same-aged groupings? Were they deficient in their emotional development? Were they psychologically stunted? Did they lose out on an indispensable piece of childhood?

In fact, research analyzing the social development of homeschooled youngsters yields several opposite conclusions. As a group, the self-image of those homeschooled is as healthy, or more so, as their schooled counterparts. They are more likely to be civic minded, spending more time in volunteer activities. They report a higher level of overall contentedness. So, if one defines the term "socialization" specifically, it seems that homeschoolers do quite well.

Full disclosure: My wife homeschooled all of our children for nearly twenty years. (She can now kick tail on *Jeopardy*.) I, too, have done my share of homeschooling. For example, some years ago, one of the little ones dropped a pencil, and I picked it up for him. My positive view of homeschooling does not imply a negative view of other education. Many fine parents, teachers, and kids are involved in public and private schools. My intention is to knock flat the cliché and baseless objection leveled at homeschooling. It is to defend those who choose that option. These parents are typically involved and conscientious. They are not unwittingly shortchanging their children's well-being.

P.S. My wife graded this for content and grammar. I got a C+/B.

Part 8

# Feelings of Failure

A paramount desire of faith-filled parents is to pass the Faith on to their children. Their hope is that their children will embrace that Faith throughout childhood and beyond.

So it is with deep distress and no little guilt that a parent watches her child suspect, neglect, or reject much or most of his childhood beliefs. The self-doubt and second-guessing disrupt not only her inner peace but her relationship with her now young adults.

While all things church may not be unfolding as Mom or Dad expected, that doesn't mean they are at fault. It also doesn't mean the story is over.

# Talk the Walk

*Dear Dr. Ray,*

*I've always believed that my actions speak louder than my words. So, as the saying goes, rather than talk religion, I've chosen to walk religion. My kids are nine and thirteen, and I'm not sure they're walking behind me.*

*Speechless*

The following saying has long been attributed to St. Francis: "Preach the gospel always, and if necessary, use words." In fact, St. Francis never said that. He was a preeminent preacher. The power of his words derived from the power of his actions. The two moved in inseparable tandem. One reinforced the other. Alone, each would not have carried the same weight.

Practice what you preach; walk your talk; values are caught, not taught; children learn what they live. These are all worthy phrases, with a large measure of truth. But they don't speak the full truth.

Most people—"people" includes kids here—are indeed more influenced by another's behavior than by that person's speech. If a picture is worth a thousand words, then images of good living are worth many thousands of words. Actions that don't match my words, to be sure, hollow out those words.

Yet actions alone are not necessarily sufficient. Words reinforce actions.

First assumption: You are older than your children. Thus, your moral conduct may be more obvious to you than to them. It takes maturity to draw moral lessons from what one sees in others. A nine- and a thirteen-year-old are still growing into moral maturity. For that matter, so are many adults.

Second assumption: Your kids are human. As such, their nature is fallen, bent toward self-interest. Yes, they can observe your example, assuming they are paying attention. Interest in your example, however, collides with their self-interest. While pulled toward emulating you, they are also pulled toward their own wants.

Third assumption: You are human. You, too, have a fallen nature, which can sabotage your best intentions to be a bright moral light. Even the holiest of saints know their light can flicker. Acting with moral consistency is a lifelong journey.

Fourth assumption: Your behavior is overall quite admirable. But does it ever resemble that of a nine-year-old or, worse, a thirteen-year-old? Try as you might, your fallen nature intrudes and sends your kids, as psychologists term it, "mixed messages." Meaning, they aren't likely to think, "Gee, Mom is so good almost all the time. But she's only human, and every so often she slips. I understand. I, too, have that trouble."

A child's bias is to interpret a parent's moral inconsistencies in his favor. Just ask any parent who—after forty straight days of unrattled demeanor in the face of adolescent eye rolls and "Yeah, rights"—finally erupts. Will she be rewarded with, "Oh, Mother, I'm so sorry I've pushed you to your limit these past forty days. You are a walking, talking saint to have endured so long"? Or will she be charged with, "See, you're always telling me to show you respect, but you don't show me any. If you want respect, you have to give respect"?

Some twenty years ago, I returned to the Church, determined to act in moral concert with my beliefs. I don't know if people haven't been paying attention or if I'm not as obviously holy as I think. Either way, I'm still waiting to hear, "Ray, I've been watching you for some time now, and I've been so moved by your moral witness. Can you please tell me the basis for it?"

When the opportunity presents itself, I must be ready to talk my faith too. Without a willingness to offer the reasons underlying my conduct, I could be viewed, at best, as a nice guy. God wouldn't get any of the credit.

Speak openly with your kids about why you live the way you do. It's not that you're merely trying to be a good mom. It goes far deeper than that. It all flows from your relationship with Christ.

Words by themselves don't teach durably. Actions by themselves are more potent than words. For maximum teaching, however, one needs words and actions, both moving in the same direction. To rephrase whoever said it: Preach the gospel always, and make sure your walk matches your talk.

# Prayer Aware

*Dear Dr. Ray,*

*My kids – ages six, nine, and twelve – all drift off during family prayers, more so if we go past a minute or two. I worry I'm not getting through to them.*

*Talking to Myself*

I'm assuming "drift off" refers to their heads, not their bodies. If a child wanders off physically, it's not likely his brain will stay put, unless he can bilocate. (If he can, I don't think you need be too concerned about the quality of his prayer life.)

G. K. Chesterton, the Catholic philosopher and author, said, "If a thing is worth doing, it is worth doing badly."[6] Applying that to prayer, we can say that, in itself, prayer is worthwhile, so one shouldn't refrain from prayer because he doesn't pray perfectly. Even when the mind isn't one with the words, the heart can be well aimed.

That your children aren't always one with you in prayer is not likely a sign of poor parenting. Their distractions are due more to

---

[6] *What's Wrong with the World* (Manchester, New Hampshire: Sophia Institute Press, 2021), 202.

age than to disposition. The relationship is pretty basic: Younger equals less prayer perseverance. The opposite isn't necessarily true: Older doesn't automatically equal more prayer perseverance. The mind, even the most mature, retains its proclivity to meander.

I've prayed many Rosaries, most after I married my wife. Her prayerfulness has pulled me along. Were I to gather all my attentive Rosary prayers, the total might be between ten and twenty full Rosaries. And I've been older than your kids for a long time now.

When our ten children all were under age thirteen, prayer time (and almost any other time) was marked by chaos. During the family Rosary, we sat in a circle—albeit one that kept shifting—as each of us took a turn to pray one prayer. More times than I care to count, when my turn came, I wasn't sure exactly where we were. Did I need to say another Hail Mary, or was it a Glory Be? Whereupon five or six children and one wife would snicker and compete to correct me. How suddenly they all became so prayer aware!

It's tempting to read a youngster's sloppy attention as irreverence or, worse, a flimsy conscience. Often it's neither. It's sloppy attention. Further, a child can be childish in prayer yet beyond his years in morals. Expect time—measured in years, not months—to bring better prayer perseverance.

Can you take steps to expand your kids' prayer endurance now? I pray so. Arrange the seats. You know which children make an irreverent mix. If the six- and nine-year-old amuse, distract, or agitate each other, don't seat them on the same couch. Sit between them—or would that ruin your concentration as well as any remaining sense of piety? Can they pray from separate rooms via intercom?

Stop the action. Cease praying until the kids hear the quiet as their signal to refocus. Silence can speak loudly.

And if it doesn't? Go audible: Clear your throat, snap your fingers, call the child by name, pray a little louder, set off the smoke alarm. Avoid multiplying words or lengthy reminders. Too much talk can pull everybody off track, even more than the kids do.

Rotate turns. Structured devotions—the Rosary, the Chaplet of Divine Mercy, litanies—lend themselves to this. It's much harder to drift while speaking than while listening.

Ask the daydreaming or disruptive child to pray, even if "out of turn." My high school government teacher, Mrs. Houser, called on students who looked most mentally far-off. (For months, I heard my name so often that I thought I was her pet.) This tactic can nudge a daydreamer back into the flow. It could also arouse a sibling to complain, "How come he gets more prayers than me?" Kids become hyperalert at any hint of personal injustice.

As an aside, by March in Mrs. Houser's class, I had mastered the ability to look attentive while being inattentive. My wife caught on to me by our second date.

Know when to quit. Prolonging prayer sessions to compensate for weak cooperation often leads to weaker cooperation. Longer is not necessarily better or holier. Even in prayer, the law of diminishing returns can rule.

Are you still with me?

# Asking Adolescent

*Dear Dr. Ray,*

*My sixteen-year-old son is arguing with me about God and about the Church and some of Her moral teachings. He says he wants to believe but is too confused.*

*Needing Answers*

My grandmother emigrated from Italy at age eight. Her family settled into a semicloistered Italian-Catholic neighborhood. Her parish was St. Anthony's, also the parish of a young girl named Rita Rizzo. Rita later came to be known as Mother Angelica, the foundress of the EWTN Global Catholic Television Network.

St. Anthony's was at the center of Momo's religious and social life—probably Rita Rizzo's as well. Catholic identity was planted early and remained. If the Church said it, it was so. If Momo had a question, the priest had an answer. Her faith was childlike to the end of her ninety-six years.

So it was for many believers of two or more generations past. Those days, it seems, are in their twilight. The soil for faith is littered with tons of rocks. Our society is aggressively more secular,

139

determined to shove aside God and His ways or to recreate Him in line with its ever-shifting mores.

It's the younger among us who most confront the widening chasm between childhood belief and the rebellious skepticism of pop culture. What they're taught by family relentlessly clashes with what they're taught by the world around them.

Most likely, your son's questions aren't all his own. Many have originated elsewhere: in the media, in entertainment, from friends. By a sort of cultural osmosis, others' thinking has seeped into his head. The good news: Some of the most supposedly enlightened challenges to traditional religion are illogical and shallow, thus easily countered.

A piece of illogic is "I question; therefore, the Faith is questionable." No. "I question; therefore, I question." What I personally don't understand about the laws of astronomy could fill Jupiter. Does it follow, then, that those laws are nonsense or don't exist? To better understand anything, one doesn't stop at his questions; he seeks answers to those questions.

For most of a decade, I wandered from the Church. Questions, doubts too, multiplied for me. And I nagged God: "Help me to believe." I couldn't understand: Why doesn't He increase my faith?

It's beyond question that God knows us infinitely better than we know ourselves. He knew that I couldn't live stuck in my quagmire of confusion. He pushed me to pursue understanding. So I read and listened to and queried others much smarter than I. And I received answers, good answers that had eluded my own narrow thinking.

You say that your son wants to believe. That means he is still open to where his search might take him. Cardinal John Henry Newman, a brilliant Catholic convert of the nineteenth century, said, "Ten thousand difficulties do not make one doubt."[7] That is, honest struggles do not mean abandoned belief. They may mean a desire to believe better.

Elicit your son's questions—about God's existence, science's challenges, sexual morals, however he's confused. Otherwise, he could struggle silently, holding uncertainties inside, wondering if answers exist. His questioning may be part of his making his parents' Faith his own.

One misguided counsel: "You just have to believe. You can't think your way to faith." Better to say, "You can't think *all* the way to faith." Faith and reason are not adversaries, despite modern "enlightened" claims. Yes, faith is beyond reason, but faith is not unreasonable.

What if your son has questions far beyond your ability to answer? Get help—from books, periodicals, CDs, websites, and apologetics organizations. Some solid Catholic websites offer a question or search option. They also invite calls and e-mails to a staff priest or a knowledgeable layperson. A teen's questions may stump you, but they're not going to stump everybody.

The saying is, "It's an ill wind that blows no good." Meaning, something has to be really bad for no one to benefit from it. Your son's confusion may unsettle you, but it will motivate you to learn. In helping him better understand, you too will better understand.

It is no longer my grandmother's world. Challenges to belief are everywhere, but so too are answers.

---

[7] John Henry Cardinal Newman, *Apologia pro Vita Sua* (London: Longmans, Green, 1878), 239.

# Two out of Three?

*Dear Dr. Ray,*

*My sons (ages twenty-nine, twenty-seven, and twenty-three) are all living on their own. Two love the Faith they were raised in, and one wants little to do with it. I keep asking myself, "What was different?"*

*Mixed Success*

I don't know, not without knowing your family, anyway. But I do know some general answers that might help answer your question.

How a child is raised is just one factor in how he matures into and throughout adulthood. It's a powerful one, but it must interact with others: his inborn personality, life experiences, associates, absorption of pop culture. And this is the short list.

Your boys were raised in the same family, but that family is not the same for each. It can't be. Each son has different siblings; each was raised by slightly different-aged parents; each likely left home at a different age, with siblings still at home or gone years earlier. The moral and religious upbringing was similar, but the circumstances around it were ever changing.

Even if all influences were equal, there is one you can't control: free will. God Himself doesn't mess much with that one. When all is said and taught, your children will make their own decisions to move toward or away from God. That reality can scare a parent because there is no guarantee which way a child will decide.

Is teaching the Faith little better than a coin flip then? In the end, free will trumps all? In the meantime, watch, hope, and pray?

Not at all. Children raised in the Faith are more likely than those not to absorb the Faith, even if their journey along the way is erratic. And protecting a youngster from all kinds of godless influences and seductions while his faith takes root will raise the likelihood that he'll choose well. When guiding a child, however—not something easier, like a rabid Bengal tiger—the reality is that not all of the faith-shaping lies in your hands.

Then too, free will is not static. For now, one of your children is ignoring what he was taught. That doesn't predict what he will do five, ten, twenty years from now. A treasure of free will: It is always free, always able to correct poor choices, always able to choose for God. Your son may have chosen for now, but that choice is not set in stone.

There is a converse truth. If you can't take all the blame for one child's faith stumble, you can't take all the credit for another's faith walk. Why some seek God and some don't is a mystery of God's grace. He opens eyes, but those eyes must be open to seeing. You till the soil; God spreads the seeds.

When my kids were younger, as I watched their personalities take very different trajectories, I would joke, "Some of our kids may serve the Church, and some may serve time." Yet, even if some go astray, that doesn't mean they won't come to serve the Church eventually. People do that.

# I Failed Religion

*Dear Dr. Ray,*

*I'm the mother of three children, ages twenty-eight, twenty-three, and fifteen. The oldest has left the Church. The middle one is lukewarm about religion. The jury is still out on the youngest. We so much tried to teach and live the Faith. It's hard not to feel like a failure.*

*"D–" Parent*

Do you live on a farm or in a small town? Is the year 1880? If so, your children's drift is not so common. For much of Christian history, what children were raised in, they stayed in. The family, clan, or tribe was the unchallenged teacher of beliefs, morals, and attitudes—in short, its religion.

Do you live in the United States? In the twenty-first century? Have you raised your kids here—in the past forty years or so? Then your experience is not so uncommon. Surveys confirm: Young adults are moving away from the Church in distressing numbers.

As repeated in this book, the soul-misshaping forces of our irreligious society are everywhere and relentless: television, movies, music, celebrities, academia, advertising. Even when homes try to lock the ugliness out, it can seep in like a vapor and shape how someone inside thinks, feels, and believes—often quite counter to what is being taught in the home.

Of course, young people are not equally influenced. God's grace, free will, personality, and circumstances—all interact to move a child to hold more or less tightly to the Faith. Nonetheless, many fine parents feel what you are feeling: a profound disappointment and a sense of failure that their offspring don't have a deeper sense of God's presence.

Today's parenting has been muddled by "psychological correctness." That is, there are psychologically correct ways to talk to children, reason with them, discipline them—in short, raise them. Reflect an empathic I-message, apply well-timed positive reinforcement, construct a win-win scenario, design a one-of-a-kind sticker system—and a child can be shaped like clay. A good psychological outcome is foreordained.

While useful for some kids—mostly those who could raise themselves—psychological correctness pulls many well-meaning moms and dads into a futile cycle of tentativeness, second-guessing, and guilt. In the end, it offers no guarantee of a well-adjusted youngster.

Among religious parents, a parallel notion is spiritual correctness. It says: Do the spiritual good things—attend daily Mass, say the family Rosary, confess regularly, pray together, read the lives of the saints—and you will raise a saint.

Don't misread me. All these are faith-nurturing practices that raise the likelihood of raising a saint. But they are not guarantees. And when a parent believes they are, if a saint doesn't ultimately come to be, the doubts do: What more could I have done? What did I miss? Where did I fall short? Did I compromise too much with the culture? Was I too Catholic? How could I go so wrong?

Many, if not most, conscientious parents did little or nothing wrong. They imparted the Faith as well as they could. Not having God's omniscience, they lived and taught as fallible humans.

Suppose, though, that God had been beside you every day, whispering precise instructions into your ears. That would guarantee a God-seeking young person, wouldn't it?

During presentations, I often ask parents to answer a series of questions with a simple yes or no.

Is there a God? Yes.

Is Christ God? Yes.

Was He sinless? Yes.

Could He perform miracles? Yes.

Did He have a perfect understanding of human nature? Yes.

Pausing, I then ask: Could He get most people to follow Him?

As a pensive silence drifts through the group, they answer no. My last question: "If the God-Man Himself didn't convert most, why do we think we can do better?"

In the television miniseries *Jesus of Nazareth*,[8] Mary Magdalene meets Jesus in the garden immediately after the Resurrection. He instructs her to go and tell His disciples that He is risen. Upon arriving at the room where the apostles are hiding, Mary Magdalene, barely able to contain herself, reports, "He is alive. I saw Him. He told me to tell you."

Mary receives a flat stare from St. Peter and a "women's fantasies" comment from St. Thomas. Whereupon she erupts, "Was His death a fantasy? I saw Him die." Regrouping, she finishes, "He told me to tell you, and I have done so." Slamming the door, she storms away.

The scene offers a lesson for faithful parents. Jesus told you to raise your children in the Faith, and you have done so. Now

---

[8] *Jesus of Nazareth*, TV miniseries, directed by Franco Zeffirelli, 1977.

it is their life and their free choice to believe. God asks us to be faithful, not necessarily successful.

Though you have no assurance that all your faithful years will add up to a faith-filled young adult, you do have other assurances:

1. The more faithful a parent, the more likely the kids will follow.

2. Of those who leave or outright reject the Faith, some will one day return, more believing than ever. They were given truth to return to when finding society's ways deficient.

So you've given yourself a D−, but the semester is far from over.

Part 9

# New-Time Religion

There's a new brand of agnostic thinking on the rise. The old brand said, "I don't know if God exists, so I might as well live as I please." The new brand says, "God exists, but He thinks a lot like me."

This new thinking allows its adherents to believe religious- and psychological-sounding clichés that serve the self. And to the extent that others hold to my line of thinking, I am validated. The numbers say so.

With a little scrutiny, the trendiest religious notions will unravel, allowing more godly thinking to enter.

# Spiritual, Not Religious

*Dear Dr. Ray,*

*My sister has little to do anymore with the Catholic Faith, in which we were both raised. When the subject comes up, she says, "I'm spiritual, not religious." What do I say?*

*The Religious Sister*

Some declarations spread because they soothe the human psyche on many levels.

1. They sound smart. The words alone seem to offer both a pithy and a profound insight.
2. They sound superior. They profess a "more genuine, enlightened" way to be.
3. They sound self-evident, beyond dispute. They need no scrutiny as to how much sense they truly make.

At their core, such declarations are platitudes—superficial but with little substance. They are verbal viruses that multiply rapidly through the cultural body because they suit the self.

People in counseling often introduce themselves with traits. "I'm a passive person." "My spouse is aggressive." "My child is stubborn." To move therapy forward, I must put specifics to the generic.

"What exactly do you mean by *'passive'*? Give me some day-to-day examples." "What, in particular, makes you think your child is stubborn?" In other words, I pursue the what, where, and how of the descriptions. Only then can I get a better picture of the why.

When your sister proclaims, "I'm not religious; I'm spiritual," she's relying on two words that beg for clarification. So, like a good therapist, ask her, "What do you mean by 'religious'?" "If you were religious, what would you be like?" "What is your image of someone who is religious?"

Ask her for the meaning of "spiritual." "What makes a person spiritual?" "Are there different kinds of spiritual?" "How does being spiritual show itself?"

Don't argue or challenge contradictions. Your intent is to hear and understand exactly how your sister is using those words. In explaining herself to you, she may also explain herself to herself. Sometimes, only by saying things out loud do we hear whether we make sense.

If your sister is defining these two words as many do, she's doing so quite narrowly. For example, to her, "religious" may mean "following rules." Not only that, but following rules made by people she considers hypocritical or judgmental. Or "religious" may imply rote, unthinking actions with little heart behind them.

"Spiritual," to her, is the loftier word. It speaks of a connection, however loose, to another power, perhaps a higher one. What's better, the power commands little obedience to traditional morals or worship.

"Spiritual" is among the mushiest words in the lexicon. It can mean whatever one wishes it to mean. The spiritual one sets his own terms; therefore, he follows them to the letter.

Suppose I announce to my wife, "Honey, from this point forward, I want to be more 'marriage minded' and less married. I think the expectations and structure of marriage are impediments to our true selves. Let's not stifle our relationship with rules. As long as we think lovingly about one another, we don't have to do all the nitty-gritty of actual loving."

Pretty much, I would declare myself free from the actions, responsibilities, and, yes, sacrifices crucial to a good marriage. Come to think of it, more people do seem to want the marriage mind without the marriage. But somehow, I don't think my wife would be enamored with this philosophy.

"I'm spiritual, not religious" is what logicians would call an either-or proposition. That is, one is either spiritual or religious but not both. To a believer in the God of the Bible and His plan of salvation, "religious" and "spiritual" represent a both-and proposition. They exist together, part of the same truth. Religion puts the substance to the spiritual. It defines worship and morality. The words overlap so much that they are nearly interchangeable.

Next time your sister says, "I'm not religious; I'm spiritual," you can ask, "Can someone be both religious and spiritual?"

# Am I Good or What?

*Dear Dr. Ray,*

*My brother no longer pays much attention to the Catholic Faith, in which we were both raised. He declares, "I'm a good person. That's how God will judge me." In fact, he is a pretty decent guy.*

*Just Okay Brother*

Several decades ago, some expert types advanced the notion that a positive self-image is key to psychological adjustment. A tsunami of purported benefits follows from thinking well of oneself—academic success, achievements, better relationships, inner peace. Likewise, the negatives recede—self-doubt, social conflicts, unhappiness, legal troubles. On paper, it all sounds good. Raise self-esteem, and you raise life's desirables and lower its undesirables.

Reality judges theories and notions. The self-esteem movement has seen most of its predicted benefits unravel in the face of closer scrutiny. Put bluntly, self-esteem isn't related to a whole lot.

Even so, faith in the need for high self-esteem has locked itself into the popular mindset. "You can't like others if you don't like yourself." Children, early on, are taught the mantras: "I'm special."

"No one else is like me." "I'm one of a kind." (Stickers and trophies for everyone!)

At one level, Christians would agree with such self-assessments. Every person has worth, inherent and infinite, because every person is made in God's image. True self-esteem, however, comes from divine declaration, not human.

Some years ago, a survey presented a list of high-profile people and asked respondents, "How likely are these people to go to Heaven?" The number-two vote getter was Oprah Winfrey, with 66 percent of people believing she was Heaven-bound. Only Mother Teresa, at 79 percent, outpolled her. Eighty-seven percent of respondents, however, believed they themselves were likely to see Heaven. Conclusion? Most people think they are as holy as Mother Teresa, or more so.

Who defines what is good? If I do, why wouldn't I be in Mother Teresa's saintly league? I'm the judge. I set the bar, one that is on level with how I'm living. My standards are as credible as God's.

Does society define what is good? I don't cheat, steal, or lie (not regularly anyway). I obey most laws, pay my taxes, and am a good spouse and parent. I even get to church every so often. Overall, I'm a good citizen. My conduct is in line with what society and the law say is acceptable.

Perhaps, but society and the law reflect reigning and ever-shifting standards, which may or may not reflect God's never-shifting standards. Abortion is legal and approved by half or more of the population. Does that number it among moral goods? Premarital sex, out-of-wedlock pregnancies, and even adultery have become more widely accepted. Judging by the tallies, are they now morally okay? Are they no longer sins that can taint one's goodness?

"I'm a good person" routinely leaves unsaid, "by comparison." If I do less bad than others do, I'm better, relatively speaking. This is the "I'm not on drugs" measure. Given what others are doing or what I could be doing, I look pretty good. God should be grateful.

If God assessed goodness as humans do, most of us would be on fairly solid moral ground. Instead, He's made it abundantly clear that we are all sinners in need of His salvation, mercy, and grace. Not that we are bad people. Quite the contrary, we are infinitely valuable souls. Still, God wants us to be good by His terms, not ours.

Because of my self-interest, I can't accurately judge my self-worth. Real self-esteem comes from God's judgment, not mine.

Ask your brother a few questions the next time he asserts that God will approve of his conduct on Judgment Day. Who decides what is good? Do you believe that everything society declares as good really is? Where would you and God disagree about what is good? Does God judge us on what we call good or on how much we love Him and others? Jesus says no one can be good apart from Him; are you saying your goodness comes from Him?

The final word comes from our Lord. When addressed as "Good Teacher," He answered, "Why do you call me good? No one is good but God alone" (Mark 10:17, 18).

# Good Enough for Me

*Dear Dr. Ray,*

*What can I say to my twenty-one-year-old, who insists on living how he wants and tells me, "God loves me the way I am"?*

*Love Him*

Say two things: Yes, He does; no, He doesn't. As the preachers preach: God loves us as we are, but He loves us too much to leave us as we are.

Your son is right, but not in the way he thinks. God does love him, with his sins and all. God loves him because God is love. His love is unconditional: It does not rise and fall with your son's conduct. God loves him not because of how he acts but because of who he is—a child of God.

So tell your son, "You're absolutely right. God does love you." Then follow with "You're absolutely wrong too. God doesn't love the wrong that anyone does." His nature can't embrace sin. And God defines sin; we don't.

Tell your son that, as his mother, you love him, no matter what, always. But you could never love or accept anything he does that could hurt him. If he's living in ways that are foolish, self-destructive, or wrong, how could you love that? How could you want that for him? That wouldn't be love; it would be misguided, blind acceptance. Your son declares, "I don't think I'm doing anything wrong." No doubt he doesn't, or he's trying to convince himself that he doesn't. (Never underestimate the morals you laid down for years, likely still buried somewhere deep within him.) I may proclaim, "I'm talented enough to play major league baseball." Indeed, I can proclaim all sorts of things, all real in my head. That doesn't mean they are real.

The modern mindset has taken the phrase "Don't judge me" to an absurd extreme. Not only do people bristle at anyone's judging their conduct as right or wrong; they don't like having God do it either. As they see it, He needs to accept who they are, and that includes what they do. God is no longer Lord of the universe. He is an indulgent uncle who smiles and nods permissively at how His nieces and nephews behave, whenever and however. That's a comforting image. It's not real. It's one of our own making.

"God loves me the way I am" is one of a long list of self-created God qualities. Another is "God wants me to be happy." Yes, He does, if that means living the way He knows is best, as He designed us. He doesn't want me to be happy if "happy" means sinning. Chasing sin to find contentment is like playing with a scorpion. It's only a matter of time.

"God understands me." Of course He does. He understands us infinitely better than we understand ourselves. Many of us spend our whole lives trying to see ourselves more clearly, and even so, our vision is clouded, blurred even, by strong self-interest. Because God understands me doesn't mean that He agrees with me.

"God knows my heart." True, He knows my innermost being. He also knows when and how my heart may be misleading me, especially away from Him. "Heart" has become another word for "feelings." And feelings are notoriously fickle. Because I feel something is right and good doesn't mean it is. God, not my heart, is the judge of right and good.

All this may sound sensible to you. How could your son disagree? Because right now, he may just want to live his way, with the rationale "God loves me the way I am." He may not fully believe it, only enough to pacify any conscience vibrations.

Reasoning with your son will likely meet defensiveness. He's protecting his ways and himself. Nevertheless, don't conclude you didn't reach him. Bits and pieces of your thinking could sneak in and sit for his later rethinking.

That's how most of us change our minds and lives — bit by bit, better by better.

# Misdirected Wrath

*Dear Dr. Ray,*

*I've heard Christians say, "I'm mad at God" after something bad has happened to them. That has always bothered me, but I'm not sure why.*

*Upset*

I started college on the engineering track. Mathematics was integral to my coursework. Its equations have, for the most part, faded from my recollection. A general principle, though, has stuck with me: To correctly solve any formula, one has to have as many equations as one has variables.

God alone knows every single variable involved in any life trouble — past, present, and future. He has complete knowledge of all the complexities. Without His help, we are barely first-year students in our understanding and are going to come to some wrong conclusions.

One definition of anger: People (or life) are not acting as I would like them to. To be angry at God is to say, "God is not acting as I would like." Either, "I see all this as clearly as God does, and I don't agree with Him," or, "I may not understand everything, but what I do understand, I don't like."

Some anger at being mistreated by life is understandable. And since God is the author of all life, the emotion is sometimes directed at Him. The emotion is misdirected, however. It arises from a faulty view of God's nature.

God isn't like some ancient mythological deity who flings lightning bolts at people who irritate Him. He doesn't play cosmic chess with them as the pawns. God *can't* create evil or wrong, as it is completely contrary to His being. Therefore, to be angry at God is to blame Him for something He didn't do. It's getting the main variable in the equation wrong.

"God may not have caused my troubles, but He could have prevented them." God can prevent or stop anything. So why doesn't He? What does He know that we don't?

My son Andrew was born with a cleft lip and palate, requiring several operations. Around age two, he needed blood drawn for an upcoming surgery. Because he was so young, his veins were thin and buried. Repeated needle sticks riled Andrew to scream and struggle against the restraining nurses. Because he didn't know who his assailants were, his fear magnified his pain.

Finally I said, "I'll hold him for you." As the nurse continued to probe, Andrew looked up at me—his father and protector—with eyes that said, "Daddy, why are you letting these people hurt me?" All I could think was, "Andrew, if you only knew what I know."

How often does God think, "If you only knew what I know?" Getting angry at God for what we don't know, can't foresee, and barely comprehend is, in a sense, acting like a spiritual preschooler. We believe that what little we see for the moment is all there is or will be to see.

Aiming anger Heavenward may speak a sense of spiritual entitlement. "I've been faithful. I've always tried to do what God wants me to do. And then He lets this happen to me." Or, "I've played by God's rules. I've kept up my end of the relationship. And this is how I'm rewarded."

Living God's way is its own reward, now and forever. We aren't in a position to set the terms on exactly how life should treat us. That's not what this earthly existence is all about.

Notice, though, that my anger at God is more intense when something bad happens to me. When similar misfortunes befall another, except someone I know and love deeply, I don't react as strongly. My God-aimed ire is more acute when life hurts me personally.

Anger has both a thinking and a feeling piece. When the feeling rules, we seek someone or something to direct that feeling toward. When no person is seen as responsible for our pain, when faceless life seems to have conspired against us, it is tempting to see God as somehow orchestrating it all. My emotions are telling me so.

That is when good thinking must talk sense into my emotions. God isn't to blame. Nor is He there to stop every pain. Was Jesus angry at His Father for not alleviating His suffering? No, He understood the suffering to be for a greater purpose.

God's infinite goodness is ever ready to bring healing from hurt, good from bad, growth from pain. We have to cooperate with Him. And cooperation begins by not being angry at God.

# About the Author

Dr. Ray Guarendi is the father of ten, a clinical psychologist, an author, a public speaker, and a nationally syndicated radio and television host. His radio show, *The Doctor Is In*, can be heard weekdays on EWTN Radio and Sirius/XM satellite radio. Dr. Ray's national television show, *Living Right with Dr. Ray*, is entering its fourteenth season. His many books include *Raising Upright Kids in an Upside-Down World*, *Living Calm*, and *Thinking Like Jesus*.